SECRET YORK

Paul Chrystal

AMBERLEY

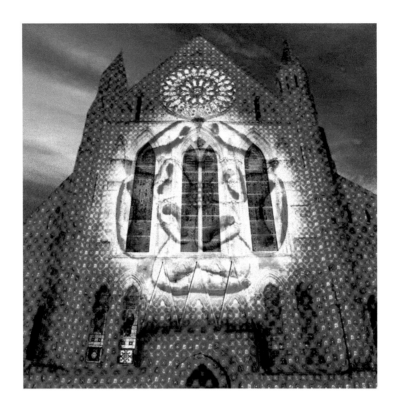

York is, of course, the guide-book man's paradise, and not without good reason, for if you want the past, here it is, weighing tons.

JB Priestley, *English Journey*, 1933

To Anne

First published 2014

Amberley Publishing
The Hill, Stroud, Gloucestershire, GL5 4EP
www.amberley-books.com

Copyright © Paul Chrystal, 2014

The right of Paul Chrystal to be identified as the
Author of this work has been asserted in accordance
with the Copyrights, Designs and Patents Act 1988.

ISBN 978 1 4456 4051 8 (print)
ISBN 978 1 4456 4084 6 (ebook)

British Library Cataloguing in Publication Data.
A catalogue record for this book is available from the
British Library.

Typesetting by Amberley Publishing.
Printed in Great Britain.

Contents

Acknowledgements

As usual, many people have been kind and generous enough to help with this book and, in so doing, make it all the better. They include John Potter, who gave permission to use the stunning photograph of the illuminated Minster that graces page 2 (for for more of his work go to http://www.jpotter-landscape-photographer.com/); Steve Lewis and Anne Wood at *The York Press* for allowing me to plunder their archives again; Tassandar@midlandsheritageforum for the fascinating photograph of Terry's Clock on page 65; thanks to Sarah Wells, Bettys and Taylors of Harrogate Ltd; Mark Sessions for permission to use the photo on page 7, originally published in Joe Murphy's *New Earswick: A Pictorial History*

Other Books on York and the Surrounding Areas by Paul Chrystal

Knaresborough Through Time, 2010; *North York Moors Through Time*, 2010; *York Then and Now*, 2010; *Tadcaster Through Time*, 2010; *Northallerton Through Time*; *Villages Around York Through Time*, 2010; *Harrogate Through Time*, 2011; *Vale of York Through Time*, 2011; *In and Around York Through Time* 2011; *York Places of Learning Through Time*, 2012; *A to Z of Knaresborough History Revised Ed*, 2011; *Chocolate: The British Chocolate Industry*, 2011; *In and Around Pocklington Through Time*, 2012; *The History of Chocolate in York*, 2012; *Selby and Goole Through Time*, 2012; *Fry and Cadbury Through Time*, 2012; *Confectionery in Yorkshire Through Time*, 2012; *York Industries Through Time*, 2012; *In and Around Easingwold: The Passage of Time*, 2012; *The Rowntree Family of York*, 2013; *A–Z of York History, Fonthill, 2013*.

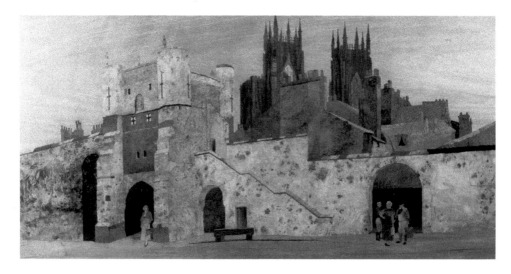

This rare painting hangs in the infamous Bettys.

Introduction

York is one of the most historically interesting cities in Europe. Most of York's history is well-known by residents and visitors alike. There is, however, still much that is shrouded in mystery, much that has unintentionally lain secret, bits of the history of York fewer people are that familiar with. This clandestine aspect of York's history has not been kept secret on purpose, it has just been forgotten about or is difficult to unearth and, for that reason, is not always included in the standard histories of or guides to the city. *Secret York* exposes and unravels some of the more arcane and less savoury aspects of the city's chequered past.

The book is in the form of a tour of the city, taking in these unobtrusive and surprising places, people and events in a journey you can join, leave and rejoin as you wish.

Our mystery tour takes in a host of characters, such as Constantine, Ivar the Boneless, Guy Fawkes, Dr Slop, hangman Mutton Curry, Dick Turpin, God's own arsonist John Martin and celebrity, Blind Tom – some of these characters were out and out villains, or not quite the respectable burghers we usually assume them to be. You will visit Bitch Daughter Tower, Bettys Briefing Room, the Ice House, the hidden, now closed, Poor Clare convent, Tyburn gallows, the Doom Window and the Cold War nuclear bunker. You will learn about the massacre of York's Jews, how Margaret Clitherow suffered a slow, painful death for her religion; how the Rowntrees were involved in racism and industrial espionage; how Joseph Terry had a foul temper and how the Suffragettes smashed the windows at a York school. In short, *Secret York* is a uniquely revealing historical guide that exposes much that has remained 'secret' over the last 1,600 years.

A number of the illustrations were mined from the superb archive at *The Press* in York. The book owes much to *The Press* and, in particular, to the hard and diligent work of Anne Wood, who helped exhaustively with the images. The text is all mine and does not reflect the views of *The Press* in any way. Any errors in the text and captions are entirely my responsibility.

New Earswick, Haxby Road & Rowntrees

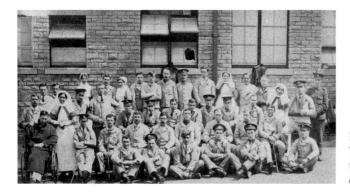

Recuperating the First World War injured in Rowntrees – the dining-room building was converted into a hospital.

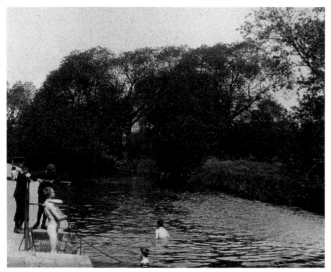

Old Yearsley Baths near Yearsley Bridge on the Foss – the riverbed was simply bricked over. It opened in 1859, but was hugely unpopular with girls and women because the men bathed naked there, as this splendid Evelyn Collection photograph clearly shows. Up the road at the Lock Keeper's Cottage, a policeman rented the place for 1s a week, in exchange for supervision of the lock and the bathers and feeding the swans. In 1909, Joseph Rowntree built and donated the Yearsley Road swimming baths next to the Haxby Road factory for the people of York. © YAYAS

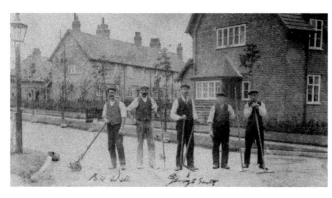

New Earswick estate workers around 1910.

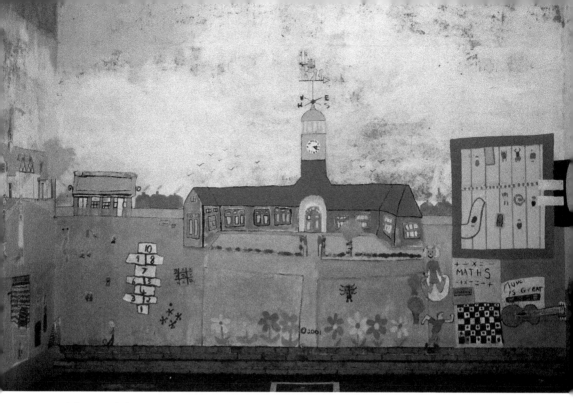

Part of the mural showing New Earswick Primary School, painted by pupils.

New Earswick and Nazi Ideology

In developing the garden village of New Earswick, Joseph Rowntree was heavily influenced by Ebenezer Howard's (1850–1928) vision of a kind of utopian city where citizens lived in harmony with nature, as expounded in his 1898 *Tomorrow: A Peaceful Path to Real Reform*, retitled *Garden Cities of Tomorrow* in 1902. Howard's towns were to be slum free, and managed and financed by the residents who enjoyed a financial interest. They combined the best of town and country life. Equal opportunity, good wages, entertainment, low rents, beauty and fresh air were the aims: we can recognise all of these factors in Joseph Rowntree's New Earswick. Howard's humanism and his progressive vision were influential in other countries too, not least in Germany where the German Garden City Association, '*unseren Deustschen Vettern*' as the people of the village welcomed them on their visit in 1909, flourished. There is, however, a sinister side to the story. Theodor Fritsch (1852–1933) claimed to be the originator of the garden city concept, anticipating Howard in his 1896 *Die Stadt der Zukunft (The City of the Future)*, the 1912 second edition of which was subtitled *Gartenstad (Garden City)*. Fritsch took a highly racist perspective – completely at odds with Howard's – that later contributed to Nazi ideology and made Fritsch something of a prophet of Nazism. His other work, mostly published in his journal, *Hammer*, was anti-Semitic and supremacist. Despite the fact that, in 1910, German eugenicists were sitting on the board of the GGCA and the long tradition of town planning and architecture was hijacked in the name of racial cleansing and eugenics, the Association rejected Fritsch. This did not, however, stop the establishment in Bremen of a *siedlung* under the Third Reich: part garden city, part half-open prison, part eugenicistic selection centre.

New Earswick Primary School and the Window-Smashing Suffragettes

The 'Open Air School' opened in 1912; it was a model of educational enlightenment: boys and girls were taught the same subjects (learning science was normally the preserve of boys) and all the windows faced south, opened to an extent of 18 feet, and were at head level to maximise natural daylight. Pupils could see out of these windows. Each child had 15 square feet of floor area – 50 per cent more than was required by the Board of Education then. Class sizes were limited to thirty pupils although, at the time in York, classes of between fifty and sixty were the norm; the trustees paid for an extra teacher to facilitate this. The opening ceremony, attended by local dignitaries led by Joseph Rowntree, attracted a number of suffragettes who threw bricks through the windows. Miss Violet Key Jones, a prominent and active member of the York branch of the Women's Social and Political Union (formed nationally in October 1903 by Emmeline Pankhurst) jumped onto the running board of Sir Walter Worsley's car and went on to the Folk Hall to scatter pamphlets urging 'Votes for Women.'

Joseph Rowntree and Industrial Espionage

In the early days of Rowntrees, times were very difficult and the future of the company was on a knife-edge. Desperate situations required desperate measures; in 1872, Joseph Rowntree embarked on a voyage of industrial espionage, taking in London, Paris, the Netherlands, Cologne, Bristol and Bournville, paying employees of Fry's, Taylor's, Cadbury's, Dunn and Hewitt, the Quaker Stollwerk in Cologne, and Chocolat Menier in Paris to divulge their firm's production processes and recipes.

Taylor's of London, 'the most extensive manufacturer in Europe of cocoa and chocolate, mustard and chicory', suffered most – Joseph hired their foreman mixer, James French, on a trial basis for 20s per week, plus a gratuity of £5 for his recipes and £1 for his fare to York. His colleague, Robert Pearce, was taken on for 17s per week after 'imparting all his knowledge'. William Garrett was recruited because he 'had the receipt of Unsworth's Cream Cocoas', and a register of all his workmates. Henry Thomson, a Taylor's man for twelve years and understudy to a superior with three times that experience, was made an offer of 30s per week and 'a lump sum of £10 for all his receipts and knowledge'. Thomson never made it to York – perhaps his conscience got the better of him. Nevertheless, it seems that Joseph came away with a fairly complete picture of Taylor's recipes, plants, customers, wages paid and their production techniques. After subsequent visits, he was privy to their costs, budgets, sales and margins; later, and Thomas Neal furnished a detailed engineering report.

The question, 'has he any special knowledge of value?' became standard before job interviews. Similar raids took place on Compagnie Francaise, who were in the Bermondsey New Road and Chocolat Menier in Southwark Street. 'Research' was carried out on other competitors, which included Cadbury, Neave's Foods for Infants and Invalids of Fordinbridge, Chocolat Lombard and Maison Guerin-Boutron, both of Paris, Ph. Suchard of Neuchatel and the English Condensed Milk Co. of Leadenhall Street. How far this is a denial of Quaker principles and practice in business is hard to tell – the practice of eliciting privileged information from competitors for money may have been more acceptable then than it is today.

John Wilhelm Rowntree and the Exploding Bananas

Born in 1868 in York, John Wilhelm was the eldest son of Joseph Rowntree. The inaugural issue of the *Cocoa Works Magazine* in 1902 featured John Wilhelm's account of the explosion on board the Royal Mail steamer *Para*, which would have been comical were it not so tragic. He and his wife, Constance, had the misfortune to be on the vessel, which was bringing, amongst other cargoes, Rowntree cocoa back from Trinidad and Granada:

> ...there was an appalling roar ... a momentary flash followed by blinding darkness. Mrs R and myself found ourselves hurled into the air ... ships officers and crew behaved as Englishmen should ... the captain, while in the air, shouted for the Fire Brigade.

The explosion was caused by a shipment of bananas; one of the passengers was attempting to see if, by extracting oxygen from the containers holding his bananas, deterioration of the fruit could be avoided or retarded. Bananas were increasingly popular at the time, with 5 million bunches imported into the UK in 1904, up from 2 million in 1900. The result of the explosion was catastrophic, with three dead and others injured, one of whom was 'in delirium'.

John Wilhelm Rowntree's Racism and the Banderlogs

Describing a mix of chocolate business and sightseeing, John Wilhelm's Mexico diaries are fascinating, if not, at times, somewhat disturbing: the 'copper coloured' coolies were

> comely women to look at, small and graceful, and with such a carriage ... [with] strikingly refined faces in sharp contrast to chattering wooly-pated niggers with their coarse features, obtrusive manners, and overflowing conceit. The nigger is to the white what the Banderlog were to the jungle ... they are hopelessly incompetent, incorrigibly idle, overpowering in their conceit and more effervescent than the Parisians ... They are however very picturesque and the women ... carry themselves magnificently and walk like Greek Goddesses.' Copies of this were sent to Frank Rowntree 'with instructions for it to be read to Acomb Adult School on the Sunday following receipt.

John Wilhelm's use of the word 'nigger' may possibly not have been quite as offensive then as it is to modern ears. The word was being used generally in a pejorative sense from around 1900, although advertisers, for example, continued to use it for some time after. There is no mitigation, however, for the comparison with Banderlogs. Banderlogs, monkey people, is used by Kipling in *The Jungle Book*, where they are regarded as pariahs by the rest of the jungle. Their trademark song goes: 'We are great. We are free. We are wonderful. We are the most wonderful people in all the jungle! We all say so, and so it must be true.'

In Chicago, racial discrimination was there for all to see; John Wilhelm's reaction on seeing race-segregated waiting rooms is tinged with irony and, to some extent, inconsistent with his racist pronouncements above:

> I suppose coloured people are never ladies and gentlemen. It is strange that, an Englishman, from a benighted country which still supports such a medieval institution as a monarchy, should find my first sentiment on the Republican and free soil of the States to be one of indignation at the insulting inequality and injustice to a coloured race who are yet, on paper, free and equal citizens with the whites.

County Industries – the Secret Rowntrees Co.

As with other companies, normal output and service was suspended at Rowntrees during the course of the Second World War to aid the war effort. A prodigious amount of impromptu management and reorganisation went into converting Haxby Road into what was virtually a munitions factory-housed in the Smarties Block. The definitive record of this fascinating chapter in the wartime lives of the staff, board and management at Rowntrees can be found in *The Cocoa Works in War-time*, published by the company soon after the end of hostilities; here are some of the details recorded there: 13,000 square feet of floor space in the new office block was put at the disposal of 300 clerks of the Royal Army Pay Corps. The Fruit Gum Department, at the request of the Ministry Of Food, manufactured jams and marmalade for Frank Cooper Ltd of Oxford. Part of the Almond Block extension was used by York firm Cooke, Troughton and Simms for the manufacture of military optical instruments. From the Cream Department came ersatz products such as National Milk, cocoa, Ryvita, Household Milk and dried egg.

The Card Box Mill replaced its production of fancy boxes to become a main supply depot for the RASC. Northern Command. The rest centre in the dining block was a refuge for blitzed families, mainly in the aftermath of the 1942 Baedecker raid, after which it was requisitioned for five nights; a VAD hospital with 100 or so beds occupied the rest of the building. The nursery was also in there. This allowed mothers of children aged six months to five years of age to come to work. At any one time, sixty children were looked after; cots and other furniture were made by the work's joiners, and the orchard behind the dining block became the playground.

The target for CIL, set by the Ministry Of Supply, was 100,000 fuses per week, made mainly for shells used in twenty-five pounder guns; this was exceeded. By the end of the war, CIL had also turned out 4 million anti-tank mine fuses. Workers in contact with explosive powder had to protect their skin and so 'make-up' rooms were set up where special face powder and topical creams were made available. Girls and women were advised to drink milk rather than tea or coffee at their mid-shift break. The sixty men and 850 women here worked alternate day and night shifts, and were under the management of the aptly named Mr N. G. Sparkes; most of them had been transferred from production work in the Cocoa Works.

ARP work included the construction of three underground tunnel shelters in the orchard, rose garden and near the Wigginton Road entrance. The fire brigade was comprised of twenty-three full-time and eighty part-time staff, complemented by 145 fireguards. The air-raid siren was on the top of the Elect Cocoa Block – throughout the war it sounded 140 times in blasts that lasted for 209 hours in total. The Estates Department was busy digging for victory; between 1939 and 1945, 8 tons each of tomatoes, cabbage and onions, 3 tons of leeks, two tons of Brussel sprouts and 13,000 heads of lettuce, along with smaller quantities of other vegetables were produced.

One of the most productive departments in the factory was the chocolate moulding department, which was engaged in the production of various types of war time chocolate. Vitaminised plain chocolate was made for army rations and for distribution by UNRRA for the relief of starving children in Europe. Blended chocolate and vitaminised Plain York Chocolate was manufactured for prisoner of war parcels; at Christmas, these were sent out with special wrappers.

Special chocolate 'Naps' in sealed tins were supplied to the Ministry of War Transport as emergency rations for use on ships, lifeboats and rafts. Pacific and Jungle chocolate was specially produced to withstand high temperatures for troops and sailors in tropical climates. A similar type of 'unmeltable' chocolate is still produced in Australian chocolate factories today. Oatmeal Block and Fruit Bar was made for the servicemen in the Far East. US Army Field Ration Vitaminised Chocolate, known as Ration D, was specially packed for the American forces. An Army Emergency Ration Special Chocolate that was hermetically sealed in tins was also manufactured, along with special chocolate rations for use by air crew to eat after baling out.

York Fever Hospital and St Nicholas' Leprosaria

Opened in 1880 at Yearsley Bridge, it tended patients with scarlet fever, smallpox, typhoid and diphtheria. In 1902, The Bungalow, a smallpox hospital in Huntington, was opened as an annexe. The Fever Hospital closed in 1976 and was demolished in 2008. York was well served by hospitals in the Middle Ages, with at least thirty-one. The most important, and biggest, was St Leonard's on land around Exhibition Square and Museum Street. One of the earliest was St Nicholas' leper hospital. St Giles in Gillygate was set up before 1274. There was a hospital at Ouse Bridge in the thirteenth century, a Maison Dieu originally catering for the poor and for lepers.

Leprosy came to Britain with the Romans, but it was the Church in the twelfth century that pressed for the segregation of lepers from the rest of society. It was a particularly repellent disease with no cure, often presenting with rotting limbs, ending in a slow death. The bone in the nose disappears and the front teeth fall out. The Bible did not help, branding lepers as 'unclean' in Leviticus 13, 44:6. Leprosy was thought to be the punishment for and manifestation of a heinous sin, notably lust, and for that reason it was classed as a sexually transmitted infection. Heresy was another of the sins responsible. Among other punishments, lepers were not allowed to talk to anyone unless they were downwind of them. The wife of Henry I, Matilda, founded the leper house of St Giles in the Fields in Holborn in the early twelfth century and gave lands to St Nicholas' Hospital, providing a meal on the eve of the Feast of Saints Peter and Paul, comprising bread, ale, butter, salmon and cheese.

Bootham

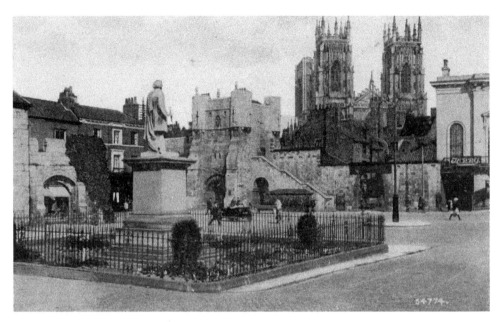

William Etty, surveying the scene in Exhibition Square at a time when Terry's used the De Grey Rooms as offices, from 1927 to 1941.

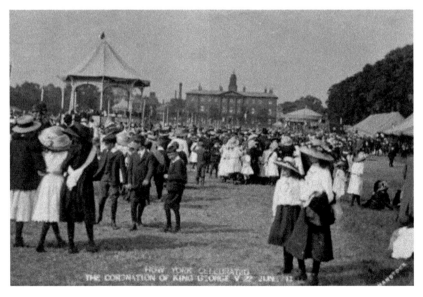

Celebrating the coronation of George V in the grounds of the York Lunatic Asylum (later Bootham Park Hospital), 22 June 1911.

Bootham Bar – 'Not Fit for any Female of Respectability to Pass'

Bootham Bar (originally Buthum, which means 'at the booths' and signifies the markets that used to be held here) stands on the north-western gateway of the Roman fortress, and was originally called Galmanlith. A doorknocker was added to the bar in 1501 for the use of Scotsmen (and others presumably) seeking admission to the city. The barbican came down in 1831 and the wall steps went up in 1889; a statue of Ebrauk, the pre-Roman founder of York, once stood nearby. Thomas Mowbray's severed head was stuck here in 1405 and the Earl of Manchester bombarded the bar in 1644 during the Civil War. The barbican was removed in 1831, due in part to complaints by residents of Clifton: 'not fit for any female of respectability to pass through' on account of the droppings of animals en route to the cattle market and its use as a urinal by pedestrians. The three statues on the top were carved in 1894 and feature a mediaeval mayor, a mason and a knight; the mason is holding a model of the restored Bar.

York Lunatic Asylum – 'A State of Filth Horrible Beyond Description'

The architect was the celebrated John Carr; it opened in 1777 in Bootham with fifteen patients, rising to 199 by 1813; its mission was to be caring 'without undue severity'. The Asylum advertised that, 'patients are admitted according to their circumstances, the terms for pauper patients belonging to the City, Ainsty and County are 8 shillings per week'. Part of the asylum burnt down in 1814, with the tragic loss of four patients and all patient records; somewhat convenient, perhaps, as the fire coincided with allegations of mismanagement, and with the rise of the Retreat, a very different, more humane type of psychiatric hospital. All staff were dismissed and replaced. In the same year, a visiting magistrate reported that the 'house is yet in a shocking state ... a number of secret cells in a state of filth horrible beyond description' and the floor covered 'with straw perfectly soaked with urine and excrement'. In 1904, it was renamed Bootham Park Hospital.

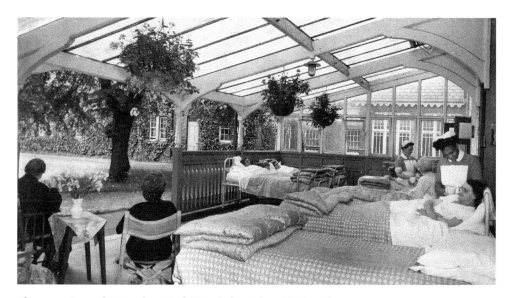

The open-air ward at Bootham Park Hospital in July 1988. © York Press

Bootham School and The Hope Street British School

The school was moved to Roman Catholic Ampleforth during The Second World War; Donald Gray, the head at the time, is reputed to have addressed the combined school as 'Friends, Romans and Countrymen'. Bootham was not the only boys' Quaker School in York: in 1827, the Hope Street British School was established and attended by many children of Friends; it was slightly unusual because, in addition to the usual curriculum, it taught the working of the electric telegraph, with the Electric Telegraph Co. supplying the instruments and the school reciprocating by supplying the company with clerks.

Marygate Tower

On the corner of Bootham and Marygate. Built around 1325, the tower was used to store monastery records after the Dissolution in 1539. During the Civil War in 1644, however, the Earl of Manchester blew it up with a mine at the Battle of the Bowling Green. Unfortunate this, but those documents that survived were salvaged by Richard Dodsworth and are now in the Minster Library. The tower has been rebuilt in 1952 and became the headquarters of the York Arts Society with a studio and library.

The Industrial Ragged School

The school was founded in 1848, moving from College Street into the Marygate premises vacated by the workhouse. In 1855, an average of eighty children attended the school in winter and forty in summer – agricultural labouring being responsible for the discrepancy. The boys were taught clog making, tailoring, gardening, and net making, the girls were instructed in domestic work and needlework. They all received three meals a day; some boarded and were occasionally sent out to work. By 1876, it had become a Certified Industrial School for Boys, continuing until 1921.

The Workhouse – 'We Found a Beast's Head at that Time Offensive to the Smell... a Quantity of Unwholesome Mucus was Attached to It.'

In 1551, part of St Anthony's Hall, one of York's Houses of Correction at the time, was used as a poorhouse. In 1567 and 1569, two weaving establishments were established for the unemployed in St Anthony's Hall and St George's House, but the goods they produced were useless. After many unsuccessful attempts, a number of the city's parishes set up a joint workhouse in 1768 to accommodate ninety paupers in a former cotton factory at No. 26 Marygate, again working with textiles. York Poor Law Union was established in 1837 and took over Marygate; hygiene left much to be desired, according to this 1839 inspection triggered after an outbreak of food poisoning from a vat of soup:

> In a room, however, in my opinion as a Chemist, ill adapted for the purpose of preserving meat, we found a Beast's Head at that time offensive to the smell...This room adjoins and opens into a short and very narrow yard considerably tainted with all the effluvia rising from some privies at one end... The head not having been previously cleaned, a quantity of unwholesome mucus was attached to it.' The Guardians nevertheless concluded that the soup had made inmates ill because 'the usual quantity of Potatos [sic] had been omitted making the soup too strong and rich.

The Poor Law Commissioners recommended a replacement for the Marygate workhouse, reporting 'a permanent reservoir of foul air'; the privies were 'without exception in an offensive state'. Most of the inmates were 'children, the aged and infirm and persons of weak mind'; many, if not all, were diseased and children mixed 'in the infectious wards with adults labouring under syphilis and gonorrhoea'. The paupers mocked the idiots 'as a pastime'. In August 1845, the *Leeds Mercury* reported on the women's ward in an official inspection: 'this place is used by aged idiots, women and children, and besides being of limited extent, it has only one privy, with an open cesspool'. In 1849, a new union workhouse was built on Huntington Road, housing 300 inmates. Different inmates were separated by a network of walls, including one specifically for unmarried women and one for 'female idiots'. There was also a washhouse, laundry, and the mortuary. On the men's side were an oakum-picking shop, carpenter's shop, stone yard, and a coach house. In 1930, the workhouse became a Public Assistance Institution, while part of the building became of York City Hospital. In 1946, it was renamed the Grange and, in 1955, became St Mary's Hospital. This closed in the late 1970s and the buildings were converted into student accommodation.

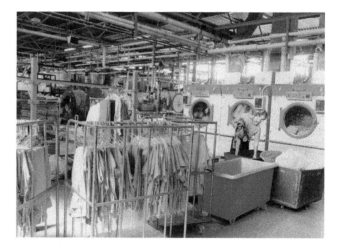

The rarely seen laundry at Clifton Hospital. © York Press

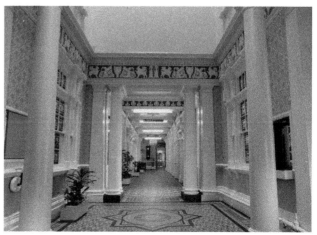

A view of the fine and elegant interior of the Bootham Park Hospital. © York Press

Goodramgate

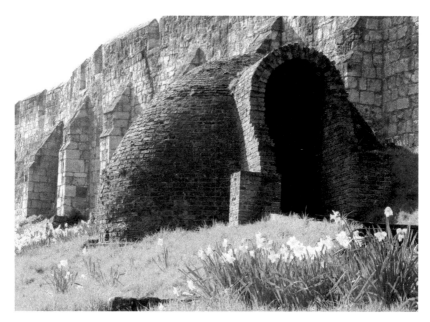

The Ice House.

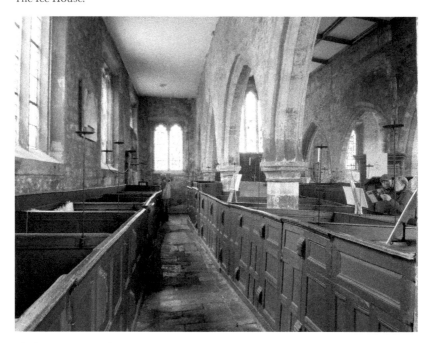

The box pews in Holy Trinity church.

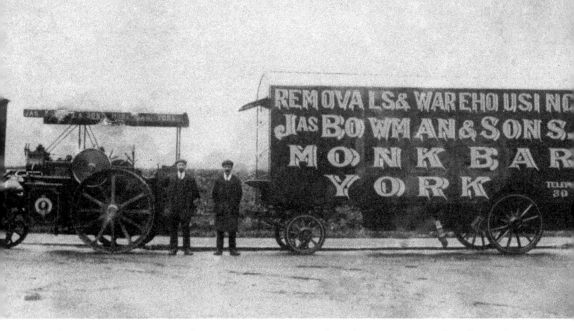

Early moves with steam power by James Bowman & Sons of Monk Bar. Quite coincidentally, another James Bowman, one of the world's leading countertenors, was awarded the 2010 York Early Music Festival Lifetime Achievement Award at the National Centre for Early Music in York. © York Press

The Ice House

This brick-lined, vaulted, early nineteenth-century edifice, on the city walls near Monkgate Bar, was used for the storage of winter ice, which in turn would be used for the cooling and preservation of food and drink in the summer. The Ice House is accessible from the pub garden at the end of Goodramgate.

Holy Trinity

Little known, this is a treasure of a church that can be found through a discreet gateway off Goodramgate or through an inconspicuous passage off Petergate. It dates largely from the fifteenth century, but has features from the twelfth to the nineteenth century. Itðs beauties include the east window with its fine stained glass donated in the early 1470s by the Revd John Walker, rector of the church, and the box pews, the only surviving examples in York, and two boards recording the names of Lord Mayors of the city, including George Hudson, 'The Railway King'.

Bedern – A Day in the Life...

Bang goes the neighbourhood. Bedern was an unsavoury, violent and impoverished place at the best of times, with 300 people sharing just five toilets according to one report. On October 10 1868, *The Yorkshire Gazette* reported on what was probably a typical day in Bedern with this encounter between John Rohan, Patrick Muldowney, Michael McMennamy and Bridget Rohan:

Complainant [McMennamy] went out of his own house...when John Rohan went behind him and struck him on the head with a poker ... two girls were fighting at the same time ... and notwithstanding the blow he tried to separate them and then Muldowney struck him with half a brick ... and while prostrate Bridget went out with a rolling pin and gave him some rattlers on the head, and the others kicked him ... John Rohan and Molly Rohan were also charged with assaulting Thomas McMennamy, son of the above-named complainant ... the girl struck him with an iron bolt and also bit his finger.

Bedern Chapel and 'Colourful Nocturnal Habits'

For the thirty-six vicars choral of York Minster, this was their first home from 1349, tucked away down Bedern off Goodramgate. The covered way over the road was allowed by Richard II, and made it easy for the vicars to get to the minster, avoiding the 'common people'. The present chapel dates from 1370 and was used until 1650 after which time in the nineteenth century it became a 'sad spectacle of poverty and wretchedness' when divided into slum tenements, largely for Irish navvies. The priests in Bedern had been indulging in 'colourful nocturnal habits' and were rehoused in St William's College so that their behaviour could be monitored more closely. One incident involved one of the cathedral freelances hitting a man over the head with the blunt end of an axe.

The Synagogue

From 1885–1995, there was a Jewish synagogue in Aldwark.

St Andrew's

In Spen Lane, it has a fifteenth-century timber roof. The only survivor of the churches made redundant at the Reformation, at one time converted into a stable at one end and into a brothel at the other. It was also one of the many homes of St Peter's School, and is now the home of the York Brethren Assembly.

Around the Minster

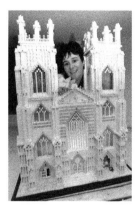

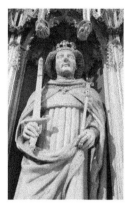

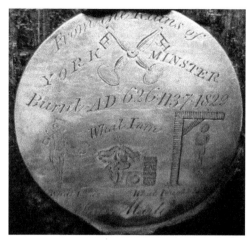

Above left: Alison Stewart enjoying the thankless task of dusting the Lego creation of the Minster's west front in 1996. © York Press

Above middle: The Choir Screen was made between 1473 and 1505, and is one of the many marvels in York Minster. Henry IV is unusual in this parade of fifteen kings of England because his face has been visibly stained with blood – this iconoclasm was carried by supporters of Archbishop Scrope, whom Henry had executed.

Top right: A wood panel salvaged from York Minster, bearing a silver medallion to celebrate the execution of arsonist Jonathan Martin in 1838.

Middle right: More plundering of Minster library books, this time less disastrously, as staff move 5,000 books (somewhat precariously) during renovation work on the library in 1980. © York Press

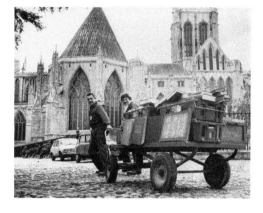

Bottom right: Verger John Daly has a close look at 'Great Peter' in 1992. At 10.8 tons, it is the third heaviest bell in the UK. Originally cast in 1845, it was recast in Loughborough in 1928. © York Press

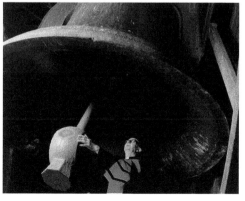

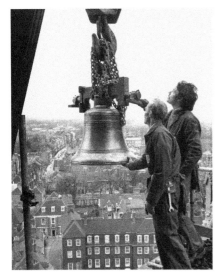

Left: 'For whom the bell tolls?' Fitting a new eight cwt treble bell high up in the south-west tower in 1980; again, John Taylor's of Loughborough did the casting. © York Press

Below: The Rose Window, courtesy of John Potter. www.jpotter-landscape-photographer.com

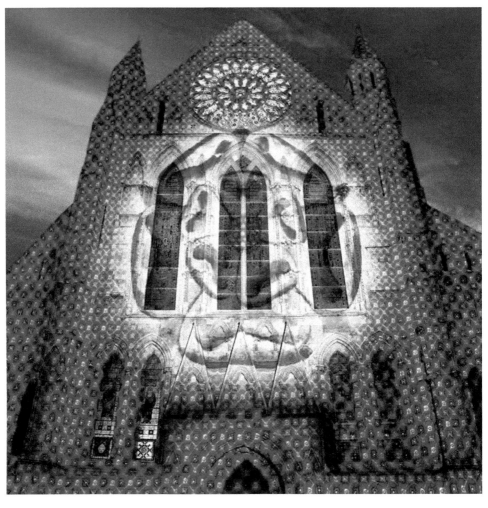

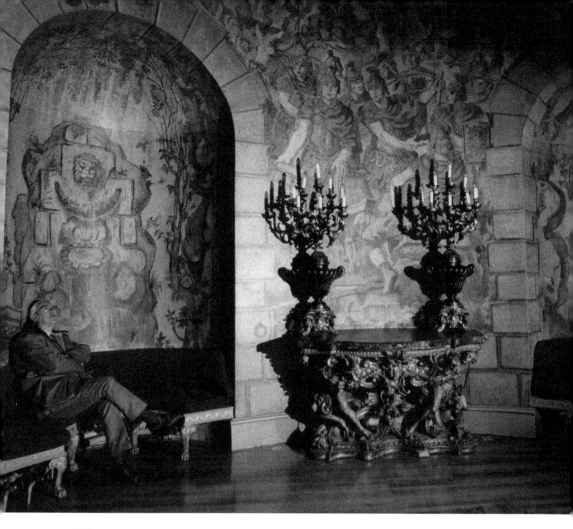

Beautiful frescoes in the foyer of the Assembly Rooms, 1991. © York Press

Right: The Chapter House
is full of grotesque carvings
like these two.

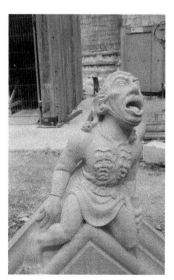

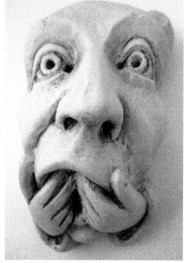

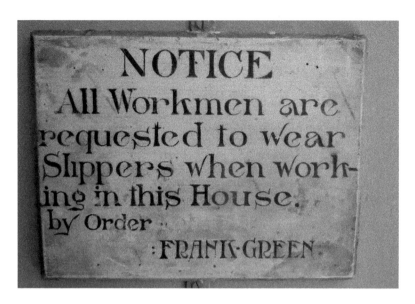

A scan of the admonitory notice can still be seen in the Treasurer's House.

Ivar the Boneless Goes Berserk

In 865, Ivar, with his brother Halfdan Ragnarsson (Halfdene), led the Great Heathen Army and took East Anglia; the following year on 1 November, they captured York. The date was no coincidence, it being All Saints Day when much of the population would have been preoccupied in the old cathedral. Legend has it that Ivar was fair, big, strong, and one of the wisest men who has ever lived. The origin of the nickname is troublesome: some say that he suffered from erectile dysfunction, or a form of osteogenesis imperfecta or brittle bone disease, while others still believe he earned it from his chubby face. Ivar was a famous berserker – Norse warriors, who in Old Norse literature are reported to have fought in a frenzied, trance-like fury (from which the word 'berserk' is dereived). Berserkers worked themselves into a rage before battle, possibly helped by drugged foods.

York Dispensary – Precursor of the NHS

The York Dispensary was a crucial part of the city's health service in the nineteenth century. It was set up to look after York's sick poor (the county hospital had no remit there), and was originally located in the Merchant Adventurers' Hall, moving to St Andrewgate and then, in 1828, to New Street. The final move was to the imposing red brick building in Duncombe Place in 1851. Its mission, as recorded in *Baines' Directory* for 1823, was 'to dispense gratuitously advice, medicine and surgical assistance, to those who are unable to pay for them'. Medicines were free of charge, and 600 or so children were vaccinated here 'without cost for the smallpox'. The Corporation contributed £5 towards an apothecary's shop and one guinea a year for five years. After thirty or so years, 42,488 patients had been seen with 28,851 cured.

Military Sunday and General Gordon

Established in 1885 by the then Dean, the Very Reverend Purey Cust in memory of General

Gordon, who was killed in Khartoum in 1884. The Sundays lasted until 1939 and were hugely popular with some people walking through the night to attend them. York's Boer War fallen are commemorated on the monument in Duncombe Place.

The Red House, Dr Slop and George Stubbs
Built in 1718, its candle snuffer is still by the front door; Dr John Burton (*Tristram Shandy's* Dr Slop) once lived there; Burton was a gynaecologist and medical author whose books included *An Essay Towards a Complete System of Midwifery*, illustrated by no less an artist than George Stubbs who had come to York (then, as now, a centre of excellence in medical science) to learn his anatomy. Stubbs found work teaching medical students in the medical school before taking up comparative anatomy and painting his famous horses. The house to the right belonged to Tate Wilkinson, the actor and theatre manager; the passage in between led to the old theatre.

Flambeaux Extinguishers
Before gas and electricity, it was a legal requirement in York for the pedestrian to carry 'light before him'. On reaching his or her destination, they would put out their torches in the extinguishers located in door niches. Three survive in York: at the Red House, in Gillygate and in Petergate.

When is a Cathedral Not a Cathedral?
When it is a minster. There is, however, very little distinction between the two. Minsters were originally, from the seventh century, any communal settlement of clergy where the act of prayer was routinely practiced. They were later established as missionary teaching, collegiate, churches, or a church attached to a monastery from which monks would go out and preach to the local community; a cathedral, on the other hand, was the seat of a bishop, his seat or throne, being a *cathedra*. Examples other than York are at Beverley, Westminster and Southwell. Minsters declined in the eleventh century with the rise of the parish church, and the name was then bestowed on 'any large or important church, especially a collegiate or cathedral church', like York. The twentieth and twenty-first centuries have seen an explosion in the number of parish churches honoured with the title 'minster'.

The Archbishops of York – from Paulinus to John Sentamu
The first Bishop of York was Paulinus in 625 – sent by Pope Gregory I to convert the Anglo Saxons to Christianity, one of whom was King Edwin of Northumbria; another was Hilda of Whitby. Egbert was the first Archbishop of York from 732 to 766. The current archbishop, the ninety-seventh, is the Most Reverend and Right Honourable Dr John Tucker Mugabi Sentamu, inaugurated in November 2005. Born in Uganda, he became a barrister, antagonising Idi Amin; he came to Britain in 1974 and was Bishop of Birmingham from 2002. Dr Sentamu is Britain's first black archbishop.

Archbishop Scrope
Executed in 1405 by Henry IV for his rebellion after Henry Bolingbroke's 1399 victory over Richard III. Henry marched on York, determined to 'wipe it off the face of the earth'. Miracles were seen in the minster, which led to Henry banning all services for a year. His death from leprosy in 1413 was seen as divine retribution for the murder of an archbishop.

Lancelot Blackburne – Archbishop and Pirate

Blackburne died in 1743. He was Archbishop of York from 1724 until his death, before which he did time as a paid spy for Charles II in 1681, and as a pirate in the Caribbean in the 1680s. He reputedly swigged ale and smoked a pipe during confirmations, behaviour typical of the man and described as follows: 'His behaviour was seldom of a standard to be expected of an archbishop ... in many respects it was seldom of a standard to be expected of a pirate'.

George Nevill: 400 Swans and 25,000 Gallons of Wine – Just for Starters

The Great Feast of Cawood was held to celebrate the enthronement of George Nevill as Archbishop of York in 1466. His brother, the Earl of Warwick, the 'Kingmaker', organised it to include 104 oxen, 6 wild bulls, 1,000 sheep, 304 veals, 304 pigs, 500 stags, bucks and does, 5,500 venison pasties, 600 pikes and breams, 1,200 quails, 500 partridges, 400 plovers, 400 woodcocks, 400 swans, 2,000 geese, 1,000 capons, 1,000 muttons, 104 peacocks, 4,000 mallards and teals, 200 pheasants, 204 cranes, 204 kids, 2,000 chickens, 4,000 pigeons, 4,000 rabbits, 100 peacocks, 100 curlews, 12 purposes and seals, 4,000 conies, 5,000 custards, 300 jellies – all washed down with 25,000 gallons of wine, one pipe of ypocras (spiced wine) and 300 tons of ale. The feast lasted seven days and fed 2,500 guests.

Kill Canon Corner

The area around the west front of the minster – notorious for its powerful eddying winds. No clergy has died here to date.

The Minster Clocks

Not many people know that, from 1750, there was a magnificent clock over the south entrance to the minster. It was installed by Henry Hindley to replace a ramshackle mediaeval clock. Henry Hindley's Striking Clock was moved to the North Transept in 1871, where it features two 400-year-old carved oak figures or 'Quarter Jacks' who strike the hours and quarters with their rods. The other wonderful clock in the minster today is the Astronomical Clock, installed in 1955 as a memorial to the Yorkshire based Allied aircrew who flew from bases in Yorkshire and the North East, and died during The Second World War. One face shows the precise position of the sun in relation to the minster at any given time, while the other gives the position of the northern stars by which aircrew would have navigated.

The Gazebo on the Minster – The Dutch are Coming

Odd as it may seem, there was an hexagonal shaped gazebo on the lantern tower of York Minster from 1666 to 1808. It was built there on the instructions of George Villiers, Duke of Buckingham and Lord Lieutenant of West Yorkshire and the City of York, to house a beacon that would be lit in the event of an invasion by the Dutch or French, our enemies in 1666. Made of wood and glass and covered in lead, it had a cockerel weathervane on top that symbolised St Peter.

Jonathan Martin – God's Arsonist

Minster arsonist, who on 1 February 1829, started the first minster fire. Plagued by depression, he had previous form for threatening to murder the Bishop of Oxford, and was committed to West

Auckland Lunatic Asylum. Some years later and living in York, Martin was irritated by a buzzing coming from the organ while attending Evensong. He hid in the bell tower until the doors were locked and shinned down a bell rope to the nave, where he piled hymn and prayer books into two bonfires and set them alight. He stole a Bible 'on the Lord's orders' and made his escape. The organ and choir were among the fixtures and fittings destroyed. Martin was arrested and tried at York Castle; the jury found him guilty, but the judge overruled and declared him not guilty on the grounds of insanity. He was committed to the Criminal Lunatic Asylum in London, where he died on 27 May 1838. One good result of Martin's action was the re-establishment of the minster police and the employment of a fire watchman-cum-constable. One of Martin's brothers is John Martin (1789–1854), the Romantic painter famous for his biblical scenes.

Peter Prison and the Key-Jangling Minster Policemen

The minster policemen originate from the office of Constable of the Liberty in 1106. In 1285, the Minster Close was enclosed by a 12-ft high wall within which the dean and chapter held sway and, until 1839, had a Liberty of their own – the Liberty of Saint Peter and Peter Prison which, in turn, had its own chief constable, constables, coroners, magistrates, bailiffs, stewards and under-stewards. After the Jonathan Martin fire of 1829, the dean and chapter decreed that 'Henceforward a watchman/constable shall be employed to keep watch every night in and about the cathedral'. Minster police predate the establishment of Sir Robert Peel's police force; indeed, Peel will have been influenced by the minster police when he visited his sister who was married to the then Dean, William Cockburn. York Minster is one of seven cathedrals in the world that have their own constabulary or police force. The others are Liverpool's Anglican Cathedral; Canterbury, Hereford and Chester Cathedrals; St Peter's Basilica in Rome (the Swiss Guard) and Washington's National Cathedral. The phrase 'taking a liberty' stems from the police here, when in the thirteenth century, the Lord Mayor persisted in entering the Liberty of St Peter to harass the residents. The Pope intervened to stop him 'taking a liberty'. Today, there are ten minster policemen; they do not carry batons or handcuffs: their non-combative role is to look after over 380 sets of keys, to provide tourist information; security for cash and fire protection. Peter Prison was reached through Peter Gate, one of four gates leading in to Minster Close or the Liberty of St Peter, a walled area around the minster; it was demolished in 1827. Jonathan Martin was one of the last detainees, by which time a report found it in 'a wretched state'. The other three gates were in Ogleforth, the entrance to St William's College and at Minster Gates.

Heathen Mistletoe at the Minster

York Minster is the only cathedral in the country that adorns its altar with holly *and* mistletoe at Christmas, despite its Druidic connections and the traditional ban on its display in churches. At York, it traditionally formed part of a service of repentance where transgressors could seek forgiveness. The priest would hold out a branch and say: 'public and universal liberty, pardon and freedom of all sorts of inferior wicked people at the Minster gates and the gates of the city, towards the four quarters of heaven'.

Mother Shipton and the End of the World

Born in 1488 (so predating Nostradamus by fifteen years), in a cave next to the River Nidd, the legendary Mother Shipton (nee Ursula Southeill) is synonymous with the art of prophecy.

Afflicted by what was probably scoliosis, and variously branded a witch and the devil's daughter, her predictions have included the demise of Cardinal Wolsey, the Gunpowder Plot, the Great Fire of London, her own death, and, as yet inaccurately, the end of the world (1881 and 1991). The earliest mention of her did not appear until 1641. This describes how, when living in York, she had predicted that the out of favour Cardinal Wolsey, who planned to be enthroned as Archbishop in 1530, would see York, but never reach the city. Wolsey got as far as Cawood Castle, and from the tower saw York Minster in the distance, vowing he would have Mother Shipton burnt as a witch. But he was arrested on a charge of high treason and died on the journey south.

The Deanery and Old Palace

Not surprisingly overshadowed by the minster, the Old Palace not only houses York Minster's unique library and archives, but also the collections department and the conservation studio. It is known as the Old Palace because part of the building used to be the chapel of the thirteenth-century Archbishop's palace. In 1810, it was refurbished and, shortly after, the minster's collection was installed there. The original library was the dream and ambition of King Egbert, a disciple of the Venerable Bede; he opened a school of international repute and started a collection of books. The librarianship then passed from 778–781 to Alcuin, one of the architects of the Carolingian Renaissance. Alcuin's collection featured works by many of the Church Fathers and classical authors such as Pliny, Aristotle, Cicero and Virgil.

Alcuin, and the Destruction of the World's Greatest Library

Alcuin (d. AD 804) spent most of his celebrated life in York, and was master of the Minster School. He went on to teach at Charlemagne's palace in Aachen, and is one of the founding fathers of European culture. He describes York in his *On the Saints of the Church of York*: '... My heart is set to praise my home. And briefly tell the ancient cradling Of York's famed city through the charms of verse.' Alcuin's extensive library was one of the best and biggest in the world and helped York to become one of the premier seats of learning in the eighth century. Unfortunately, the Vikings destroyed much of the collection in 867.

Archbishop Holgate's School and a Blockbuster Chemistry Textbook

The school is, after St Peter's, the oldest in York, and was founded as Archbishop Holgate's Grammar School in 1546 by Robert Holgate, financed by capital from the Dissolution of the Monasteries. The original grammar school was in Ogleforth and was known as The Reverend Shackley's School; Thomas Cooke taught here, the famous optical instrument manufacturer who went on to establish T. Cooke & Sons, later Cooke, Troughton & Simms, the equally famous telescope manufacturers. In 1858, the school merged with the Yeoman School when it moved to Lord Mayor's Walk. It relocated again in 1963 to its present site in Badger Hill. Chemistry teachers and old boys, Albert Holderness and John Lambert, are the authors of one of the most successful school chemistry books ever published: *School Certificate Chemistry*. Published in 1936; the 500,000th copy came off the press in 1962; the book remains in print today in its sixth edition, retitled *A New Certificate Chemistry*. Archbishop Holgate was the first Protestant archbishop in 1545, and the first to marry. He deserted both his religion and his wife when the Catholic Mary Tudor acceded to the throne in 1553.

The School of Art

The School of Art was opened in Minster Yard in 1842 as a branch of the Normal School of Design in London, with the help of William Etty. Originally in the Freemasons' Hall in Little Blake Street, it moved into the former premises of St Peter's School in Minster Yard in 1848, moving again to the Exhibition Building in St Leonard's Place, and then again to Marygate in 1949, where the roll was 594 students.

Gray's Court

Gray's Court is the oldest continuously occupied house in the country, and parts of it date back to 1080 when it was commissioned by the first Norman Archbishop of York, Thomas de Bayeux; it was the original Treasurer's House. It exudes history: James I dined here with Edmund, Lord Sheffield, the Lord President of the North, knighting eight noblemen in the Long Gallery in one evening. Sir Thomas Fairfax owned Gray's Court between 1649 and 1663, during which time he laid siege to the city. James Duke of York and Maria Beatrix of Modena, his wife, later King and Queen, stayed in Gray's Court in 1679. Elizabeth Robinson was born here in 1718: she founded the Blue-stocking Club 'where literary topics were to be discussed, but politics, gossip and card-playing were barred'.

The Royal Press

Charles I set up his printing press in 1642 in Sir Henry Jenkins' house in St Williams' College. The royal presses rolled from March to August that year and turned out seventy-four documents, including Charles' *Counsell of Warre*.

The Three Legged Mare and the Wonkey Donkey

This pub is named after a triangular type of industrial gallows that despatched three felons at once; one was in use at the Knavesmire until 1801 before it was removed in 1812. There is a replica of the 'wonkey donkey' in the beer garden of the pub in Low Petergate – there is no future in riding the three-legged mare. The pub is owned by the York Brewery, which started brewing in 1996 – the first local brewers since the closure of Aldwark-based Hunt's in 1956. The brewery's other York pubs are The Last Drop Inn in Colliergate, The Yorkshire Terrier in Stonegate and The Tap Room in the brewery itself (in Toft Green).

York Ham, Ouse Bridge Cakes and York Gingerbread

York ham is a dry-cured ham. According to legend, it obtained its unique flavour from the sawdust from the oak timbers used in the building of York Minster. However, York hams have never been smoked, although they are distinguished by the fact that the pigs' legs are long cut – they are rounded at the hip rather than squared off. *Law's Grocer's Manual* of 1949 tells us that 'In England the principal ham is long-cut, pale-dried dry-salt cured ham known as York Ham'. Other local regional delicacies include York mayne bread, which was very popular (by-laws were passed urging people to bake it) up until 1622 when spiced cake stole the market. This may have been in the form of Ouse Bridge cakes known in the eighteenth century, a type of Yorkshire tea cake. There were also Fulford Biscuits and York Gingerbread, the recipe for which was included in Sarah Martin's 1795 *New Experienced English Housekeeper*.

Stonegate

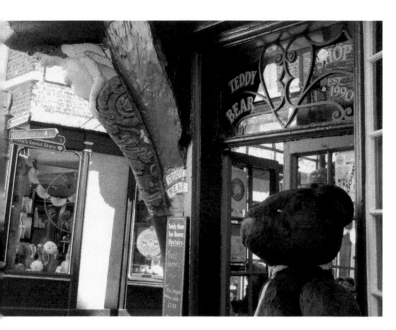

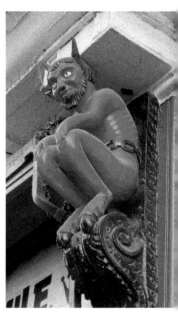

Above left: The exotic figurehead salvaged from one of the many sailing boats that used to trade on the River Ouse, just at the end of Stonegate and over St Helen's Square. Perhaps it signified that a ship's chandlers occupied the premises at some time. The twentieth-century bear seems unimpressed.

Above right and below: Four signs of York trade: the flamboyant printer's devil indicates the printing industry in Stonegate; the beautiful Minerva, the associated publishing that thrived at the top of Stonegate and in Minster Gates; the resplendent native Indian in full attire denotes a tobacconist beneath at some point; the Stonegate Bible: more printing and publishing.

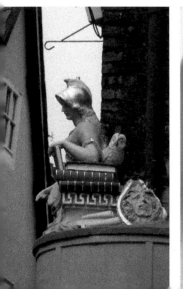

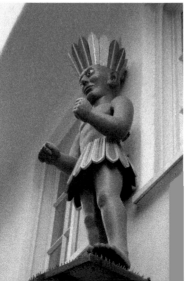

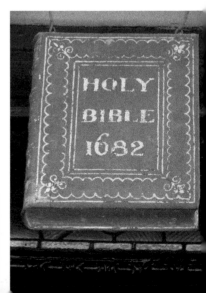

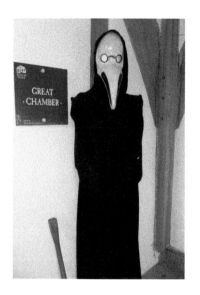
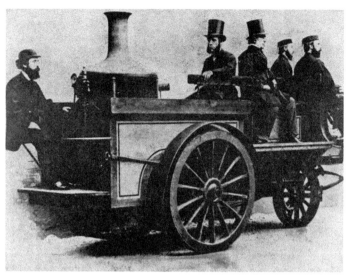

Above left: The plague doctor comes to Barley Hall. The doctors were a sort of infectious disease locum hired by plague-struck communities – the mask was filled with aromatic substances and straw to avert infection. Another plague doctor ominously stalks the rooms of the Merchant Adventurers Hall.

Above right: The steam car invented by Thomas Cooke in 1866 could reach 15mph. However, the rules of the road prohibited anything over 4mph; in frustration Cooke turned it into a boat and travelled on the Ouse at whatever speed he desired.

Below: Cooke, Troughton & Simms telescopes in use at the total eclipse of 28 July 1851 at Bue Island, Norway. From a watercolour by Charles Piazzi Smyth, the astronomer in charge.

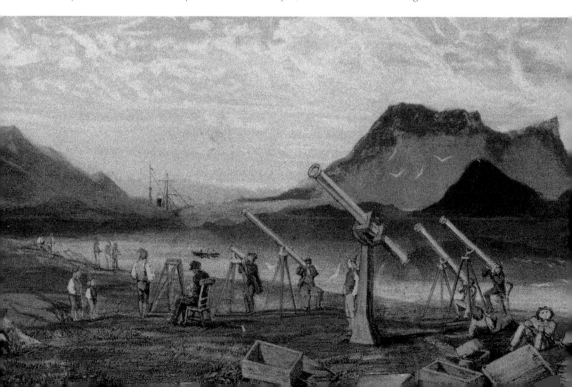

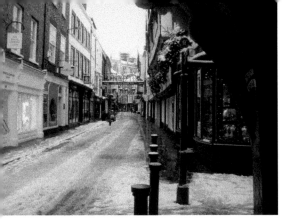
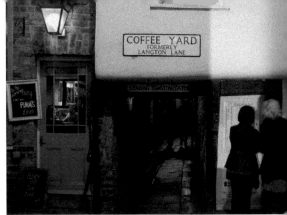

Above left: A white Christmas in Stonegate in 2011.

Above right: Coffee Yard – one of York's many atmospheric snickelways. This neologism was coined by Mark W. Jones in 1983 for his 'A Walk Around the Snickelways of York', and is a fusion of the words snicket, ginnel, and alleyway.

The Barber-Surgeons of York (Ebor), and Dentists

It was the Barber-Surgeons of York (Ebor) who were responsible for professional medical training, professional standards and practitioner licensing in York until the establishment of the York Medical Society and York's first medical school. The first Barber (Rogerus le Barber) was admitted in 1290 – eighteen years before the first recorded Barber of the London Co. The Exchequer accounts of York for 1346 tells us,

> Payments to William de Bolton and Hugo de Kilvington, Barber-Surgeons, going from York to the Castle of Bamburgh to heal the said David de Brus who lay there, having been wounded with an arrow at the said battle [Neville's Cross, 1346], and to extract the arrow and to heal him with despatch ... £6.

David de Brus was the younger brother of Robert the Bruce, King of Scotland, and victor at Bannockburn. De Brus later became King David of Scotland. At any one time, the Gild comprised twenty or so registered 'Barber-Surgeons', who cut hair, extracted teeth and performed all manner of surgical procedures. It took a seven-year apprenticeship in order to become a full member; apprentices were trained in the 'humours' in the body and the phases of the moon. The best time for bloodletting, for example, depended as much on the signs of the zodiac as anything physiological.

York Medical Society – 'Promoting and Diffusing Medical Knowledge'

York Medical Society was founded off Stonegate by seven medical men in 1832 for 'the purpose of promoting and diffusing medical knowledge'. This was intended to build on the work of the York Gild of Barber-Surgeons. The minutes of the society provide a fascinating record of rapid changes in medicine, diagnosis, epidemiology and social change, as reflected in the lectures given there over the years. The society was active in driving social change and in improving living conditions – a paper from 1842 entitled 'A Plan of Political Medicine' anticipated the ethos and practicalities of the National Health Service by over 100 years. York's pre-eminence in psychiatric medicine and patient care (as exemplified by the Retreat) is also reflected in the society's work. There were also close links with York's first medical school, which thrived between 1834 and 1858. Indeed, the annual oration and other lectures were the main source of postgraduate medical education in the city for many years. Much of the timber-framed house off Stonegate goes back to 1590 (as evidenced by the dated lead rainwater head over the entrance doors – the oldest surviving in York) although parts such as the wing known as Little Paradise to the left of the entrance, and one of the fireplaces are older still. Extensive alterations and additions took place in the seventeenth and eighteenth centuries. A dispensary and consulting rooms were developed and the west wing was added by Dr Tempest Anderson; the speaking tube from Dr Anderson's bed to the front door to address night callers can still be seen. Sales of the properties bought by Anderson's family after his death paid for the wing he bequeathed to the Yorkshire Philosophical Society at the Yorkshire Museum. The Yorkshire Law Society, established in 1786, and the second oldest Law Society in the UK, set up its library here in 1944.

York's First Medical and Surgical School

The present Hull-York Medical School is York's second medical school. The first was founded in 1834, spurred on by members of York Medical Society. Unfortunately, it was short-lived and closed in 1858, but not before it had attracted renowned teachers like George Stubbs (anatomist and later painter); John Burton (obstetrician and Laurence Sterne's Dr Slop); John Hughlings Jackson (d. 1911), neurologist and house physician to the York Dispensary – the new medical school building bears his name; Daniel Hack Tuke (d. 1895, great grandson of William Tuke), psychiatrist who trained at the Retreat; James Atkinson (d. 1839), surgeon, friend of Sterne and author of *Medical Bibliography* – the dedication of which reads: 'To all idle medical students in Great Britain'.

Resurrection Men, or Jerry Crunchers

Instances of body snatching and burking (after Burke and Hare – where victims were murdered for their cadavers) abound in York – partly because the city was on the main coach route to Edinburgh and its famous medical school. Even after the passing of the Anatomy Act in 1832, which legalised the trafficking of the bodies of lunatics and paupers between Poor Law Unions and medical schools, the 'unhallowed occupation' continued here – probably due to the opening of York's first medical school. *The York Courant* of 14 January 1834 reports that in St Saviourgate 'one Matthew Joy when questioned ... stated that he merely wanted a skull for a person who had applied to him for one, in order to pulverise it, and mix it with some treacle, to give it to a person who was subject to fits'.

The Norman House

An often-overlooked treasure in the yard of No. 52 Stonegate. It is the oldest domestic building in York and was very large, obviously owned by a man of some wealth and taste.

Thomas Cooke – Telescope Man

Thomas Cooke came to York in 1829 and made his first telescope using the base of a whisky glass for a lens and a tin for the tube. In 1837, he opened his first instrument-making shop at No. 50 Stonegate with a loan of £100 from his wife's uncle. Cooke quickly gained a reputation for high quality, and was soon making microscopes, opera glasses, spectacles, electrical machines, barometers, thermometers, globes, sundials and mathematical instruments, as well as telescopes. By 1844, he had expanded and moved to No. 12 Coney Street. The firm later developed into Cooke, Troughton & Simms, based in Bishophill, and became part of Vickers Instruments, which was later sold to Bio-Rad, formerly in Haxby Road.

Thomas Godfrey, Bookseller of 'a most indecent publication'

Thomas Godfrey was a phrenologist who dreamt up his qualifications; he opened his first bookshop at No. 46½ Stonegate in 1895, selling second-hand books 'recently purchased from private libraries'. The business was called Ye Olde Boke Shoppe (really), but it failed. Godfrey 'became dissatisfied of the apathy of the citizens and disposed of the business' – sentiments and actions that could be echoed by many an independent bookseller today. An alternative report, though, attributes his failure to the selling of Oscar Wilde's *Portrait of Dorian Gray* after it had been recalled by the publishers, thus giving 'offence to some of the good people in York by his handling of a book which was regarded at the time as a most indecent publication'. Godfrey tried again in 1904 at No. 37 Goodramgate with the Eclectic Book Co., eventually moving back to No. 16 Stonegate with a business imaginatively named The Book Co., later Edward S. Pickard. In 1982, the business moved over the road as Bleackwell's, to No. 32 Stonegate, and acquired a second shop on the campus at York University. The Stonegate branch is long closed.

The Printer's Devil and Minerva

The 'Printer's Devil' effigy at No. 33 Stonegate at the corner of Coffee Yard has been looking down on us since the 1880s, and signifies the importance and prevalence of the printing, bookselling and publishing industries in the area. A printer's devil was a printer's apprentice – a factotum. Printing was commonly known as 'the black art' on account of the inks. The Devil is indicative of the common practice of denoting one's trade with a symbol – other examples are at No. 74a Petergate: the wonderful cigar shop native American Indian from around 1800, and the Minerva, at the corner of Minster Gates, indicating a bookseller below. The reason for all this symbolism was simply that, at the time, most people could not read; even by 1870, one in three York women, and one in five men could neither read nor write, so written signs were often useless. The practice declined somewhat from 1760 when they were outlawed and when house numbering and literacy increased.

John and Grace White

John was a Stonegate printer 'over against the Star' and the only one in the country brave enough to take on the printing of William of Orange's manifesto after his landing at Torbay in 1688. White was imprisoned at Hull for his troubles until the city surrendered to William. The king promptly rewarded him with a warrant, appointing him 'Their Majesties' Printer for the City of York and the Five Northern Counties'. His widow, Grace, was the first woman to establish a newspaper here in 1718 – *The York Mercury,* in Coffee Yard.

The Golden Bible

Above No. 35 Stonegate signifies where York's leading bookseller and printers traded in the eighteenth and nineteenth centuries. The first two volumes of Sterne's *Life and Times of Tristram Shandy* were published here.

St Helen's Square, Thursday Market & Petergate

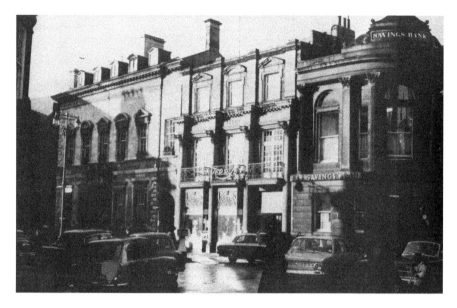

Above: St Helen's Square when the Terry's restaurant and ballroom was thriving opposite Bettys. © York Press

Below: Davygate in 1929, showing the Davy Hall Restaurant built in 1904 in Art Nouveau style, featuring a magnificent stained-glass canopy. © York Press

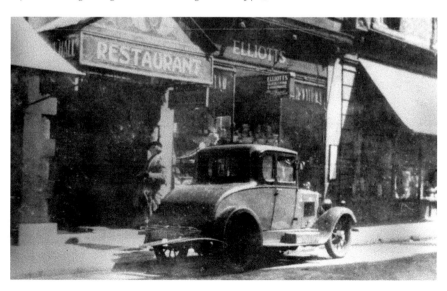

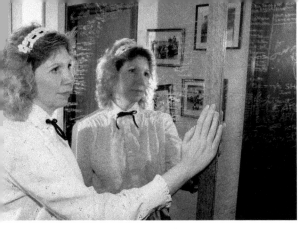

The famous Bettys mirror. © York Press

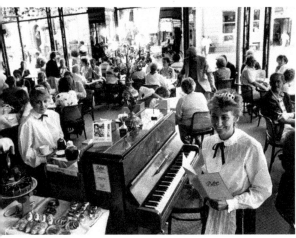

Bettys in August 1979. © York Press

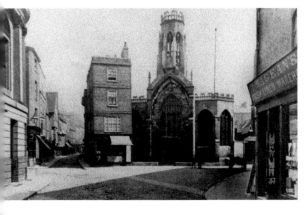

St Helen's Square before Bettys moved in.
© York Press

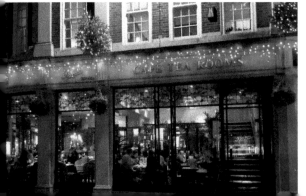

St Helen's Square, Christmas 2013.

Judges' Lodgings

A fine Georgian townhouse in Lendal, the Lodgings were a good place to stay for the judiciary attending the assizes, convenient as it was for the Assembly Rooms and Terry's Restaurant, from which breakfasts were delivered each morning. The Lodgings is on the site of a late Roman interval tower and was built in 1726 for Dr Wintringham (d. 1748), a very eminent doctor andp hysician at York County Hospital in 1746. An effigy of Aesculapius, Graeco-Roman god of medicine, guards the door. Wintringham has a monument in his memory at Westminster Abbey; he is buried in St Michael-le-Belfrey. When the Judges were in residence, they took an official breakfast on day one at the Mansion House as guests of the Lord Mayor, to which they would process in their wigs and robes. It was the official judges' residence until 1976.

Bettys Dive

On 1 February 1945, J. E. Mcdonald was the first of 600 airmen to scratch their names on the mirror at Bettys during the Second World War. Also known as Bettys Bar, it was a regular haunt of the hundreds of airmen stationed in and around York; these included many Canadians from No. 6 Bomber Group. One signatory, Jim Rogers, borrowed a waitress' diamond ring to scratch his name on the mirror. Many have returned to reflect on their efforts on the mirror, which is still on display downstairs in Bettys. Many of the signatories did not survive the war.

Who Was Betty?

So who really was Betty? The true identity of Betty has never been revealed and almost certainly never will be. Speculation is rife, however, and there have been many claimants. She may have been the daughter of a doctor who practiced in the building in Cambridge Crescent, which was to become the Harrogate Bettys, and who died from tuberculosis. She could have been Betty Lupton, celebrated Queen of the Harrogate Wells from 1778–1838 and chief 'nymph'. She might also have been the actress Betty Fairfax, who starred in the West End musical *Betty* around 1915 and to whom owner Frederick Belmont took something of a shine; intriguingly, the musical toured the country and came to Harrogate's Grand Opera House three times between 1916 and 1918. Or, just as plausibly, Betty may be the name of the little girl who brought in a toy tea tray during a meeting at which the name for the new cafe was being discussed, or of the tea lady who brought in the tea at the tea break...

Cuckold's Corner

Cuckold's Corner is the original, more secular name for St Helen's Square – as descriptive and as graphic as Grope Lane or Mucky Peg Lane.

The Press Gang in York 'to beat up for volunteers'

The Impress Service arrived in York on 18 January 1777 'to beat up for volunteers'. So angry were sections of the community that a letter was soon sent to the Lord Mayor threatening to burn down the Mansion House if the gang was not expelled. A reward of 100 guineas was offered for conviction of the author or authors of the missive, and a twelve-man guard was put on the Mansion House. Some ill-disposed citizens used the presence of the press gang as an opportunity for revenge to rid themselves of enemies by reporting scandalous and incriminating stories to the lieutenant; or to benefit financially by posing as the press gang, seizing men and extorting money from their families for release. The real gang departed on 14 February 'having picked up a great Number of hands for His Majesty's Service', as reported in the *York Courant*.

The Slave Market
A slave market is said to have existed in St Sampson's Square during the Roman occupation. Later, Bede tells us that Pope Gregory I (d. 604) admired English slaves, punning *'non Angli sed angeli'* – 'they're not Angles, but angels'. More recently in 1909, the use of slave labour on cocoa plantations became a controversial and embarrassing ethical issue for the chocolate industry, particularly Fry, Cadbury and Rowntree, philanthropists and Quakers all. During the Civil War ,Cromwell's army 'shot well nigh forty Hot Fiery bullets' into the square, one of which 'slewe a maide'. The sign on The Three Cranes pub in the square is designed to mislead – the pub is named after the lifting gear used by stallholders rather than anything ornithological.

Brown's
Founded by Rhodes Brown, an old boy of Blue Coat School, Brown's was set up in 1705 to feed and educate the very poor.

Mucky Peg Lane – Pig or Prostitute?
Off St Sampson's Square, now Finkle Street, the lane was a notorious haunt for prostitutes, which presumably accounts for the name. An alternative name is Mucky Pig Lane.

The Roman Bath
Formerly The Mail Coach, The Barrel Churn, The Cooper and The Barrel, the Roman bathhouse, excavated here in 1930, is partly visible, including its cold room (*frigidarium*), hot room (*caldarium*) and underfloor central heating system (*hypocaust*). Tiles stamped *Legio VI* and *Legio IX* have been uncovered, recording the legions that were stationed here at *Eboracum*.

The Low Petergate Indian: 'Got a Light?'
The Native Indian above No. 76 Low Petergate dressed in Virginia tobacco leaves indicates the presence of a tobacconists at some time in the past. There used to be a metal horse's head below the Indian whose nostrils used to flare with gas jets to provide a light for customers and passers-by.

Ancient Society of York Florists
Established in 1768, the society is the world's oldest horticultural society and runs the world's longest running flower show; it is held now at Askham Bryan, but before that was in Colliergate (where there is a plaque) and at Baynes Coffee House in Petergate.

Mad Alice Lane
Between Swinegate and Low Petergate, it is named after Alice Smith, a resident hanged for the crime of insanity in 1825. It also goes by the less picturesque name of Lund's Court.

Parliament Street, Pavement & Spurriergate

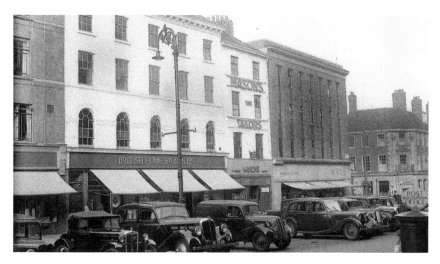

Parliament Street parking in the 1940s.

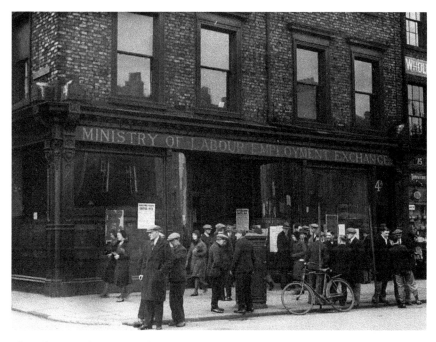

The Labour Exchange in Parliament Street in 1905. © York Press

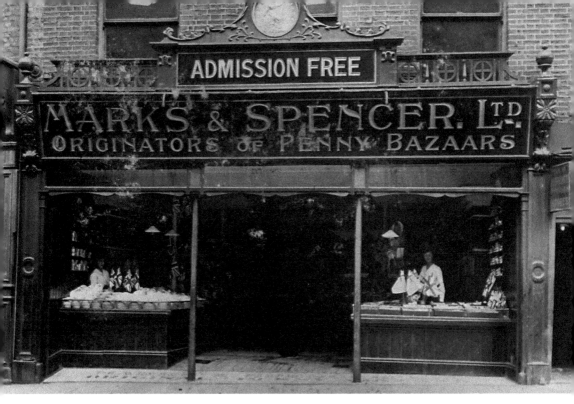

The first M&S at Nos 15–17 Parliament Street in 1901. © York Press

York's Famous Yellow Mixture – Good for Pains in the Side and Breasts

Patented by Charles Croskell (d. 1891), who ran his pharmacy in Parliament Street, selling copious amounts of the famous eponymous Yellow Mixture, highly efficacious in teething babies and for other infant ailments. His Female Pills were the best remedy for every kind of female complaint: heart palpitations, pains in the side and breasts, headache, sallow complexion, depression of spirits, feebleness and swelling of the limbs.

Pavement – Woman for Sale

A veritable menagerie and a hive of activity, all life was here. *Ye Old Streete of Pavement*, written by W. Camidge in 1893, and published by the *Yorkshire Gazette*, provides a colourful, vivid picture of activity there over the years. We read of the Goose Flags – the path in front of St Crux signifying the goose market there, boots and shoes on sale 'in Whip-ma-whop-ma-gate, where members of the "Worshipful Company of Translators" sold these commodities, old and new', and 'the basket market ... at the bottom of Colliergate'. The pleasure fairs 'at Whitsuntide and Martinmas', and the shows that accompanied them were very popular too; there were dog and lion fights 'and other shows with fat women, deformed men, giants and dwarfs, reptiles, waxworks, mechanical inventions, fortune-tellers, circuses, boxing booths', along with swing boats and hobby horses. Peep shows were particularly popular:

> their incidents stirring, and their pictures very striking ... chiefly battles ... Waterloo and the crossing of the Alps by Napoleon ... described by the showman in measured and monotonous tones in which fact and fancy were mixed up in most bewildering confusion.

On most Saturdays there were auction sales in Pavement:

Not the least interesting was the sale of a woman [in 1839]. She had left her husband through his drunken habits and ill-treatment, and in one of his mad freaks he had brought her into the Market-place ... with a halter round her neck. She was mounted on a table beside the auctioneer, who descanted on her virtues and spoke of her as a clean, industrious, quiet and careful woman, attractive in appearance and well mannered.

She went for 7s 6d, halter included, and proceeded to live with her purchaser near to Pavement. Twenty years later, her husband died and she married said purchaser; she herself died in the 1880s 'at a great age, respectable and respected'.

Camidge gives a graphic account of the near anarchy and corruption that attended elections: 'It was not unusual during the progress of an election to roll into the Pavement large barrels of ale, one end of which was speedily knocked in , and then a scene of indescribable confusion and contention ensued. Men, women and children rushed for the beer barrel, and with every description of kitchen and other utensils they sought to drink their fill, and carry off what unsteady legs, and intense excitement would allow them to get away with. It was no uncommon thing as the beer neared the bottom for someone to fall, or be pushed into the barrel.'

Pavement and Minster Yard were 'proverbial for fights' – the latter because of the ready supply of staves as: 'the Minster was at that time encircled with wood palisades ... one man ... dyed his whiskers and hair to the colour he had voted, but found himself minus of much of his hair before he escaped from the crowd'.

Camidge tells us that 'public-houses were also opened as "free houses" where an elector on producing a ticket could have a free drink'– this cost one candidate in 1830 around £1,200.

The Kew of the North

An early day, state-of-the-art garden centre run by Darlington Quaker James Backhouse in Fishergate, with 'branches' (no pun), in Acomb, Poppleton Road and Toft Green. They bought the gardens of George Telford, another celebrated gardener who, according to Francis Drake in *Eboracum*, was 'one of the first that brought our northern gentry into the method of planting all kinds of forest trees, for use and ornament'. James Backhouse and his brother, Thomas, were nationally celebrated nurserymen; their gardens were collectively called the Kew of the North. They were responsible for the cultivation of numerous rare plants, some of which James brought back from South Africa and Australasia. A particularly striking feature was a twenty-five feet high Alpine gorge built with 400 tons of rock, which led to a surge in rockeries all over the country. In 1938, the nurseries were sold to the Corporation who made them into a park; this lasted until 1946 when, sadly, it was all covered over. Backhouse had been producing catalogues long before 1821 when the second edition of their pithily titled *Catalogue of Fruit and Forest Trees, Evergreen and Deciduous Shrubs, Ornamental Annual, Biennial Plants, also of Culinary, Officinal and Agricultural Plants* was published. It was the Backhouses who first donated the daffodils to York City Council for planting on the walls opposite the station; their descendants still delight us every spring.

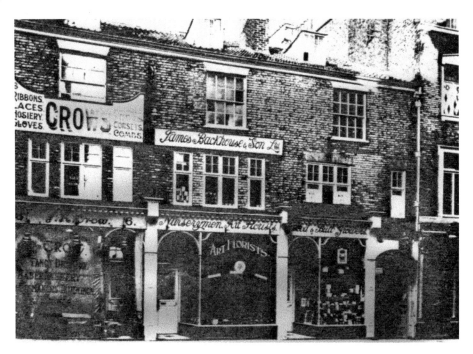

The Backhouse florists in Spurriergate in 1955; Woolworths and then Boots took over the site.
© York Press

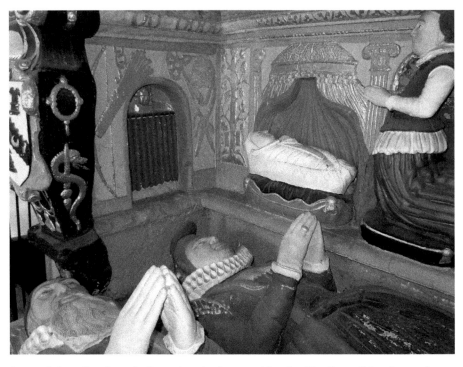

Some of the relics from St Crux church, destroyed by the City Council in 1857 and now preserved in St Crux Parish Hall, constructed from the rubble of the church.

Exhibition Square, King's Manor & Museum Gardens

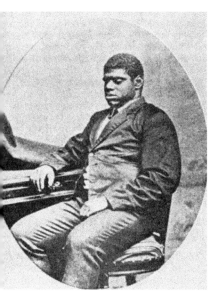

Above: Blind Tom, The Inexplicable Phenomenon.

Right: Be careful what you wish for. This is the Museum Street in 1955 on the approach to Lendal Bridge, crammed with bicycles, buses and taxis. Not much fun for pedestrians.

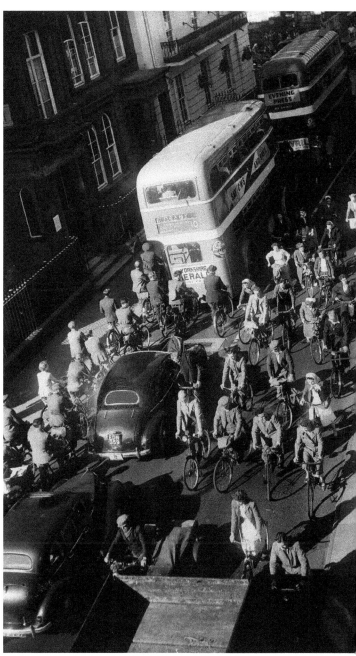

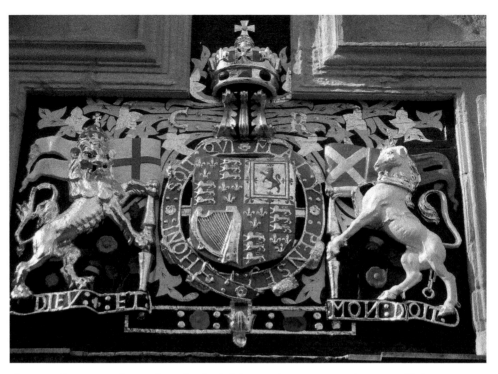

The magnificent coat of arms above the door of the King's Manor. Note the inverted 'N'.

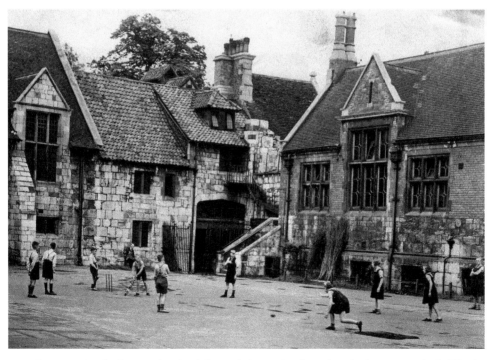

A cricket game for the boys and girls of the Yorkshire School for the Blind on 1947. The ball had a rattler on it and the umpire blew a whistle to communicate his decisions. © York Press

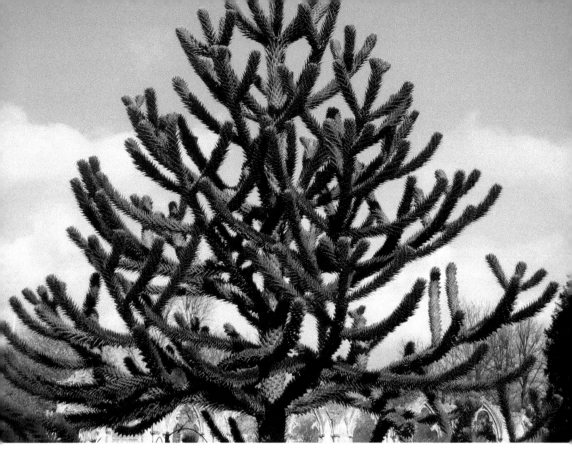

Monkey Puzzle Tree and St Mary's Abbey from the Museum Gardens, still a Botanical Gardens. The land was given to the Yorkshire Philosophical Society on condition that botanical gardens were established on the site. Originally, from the 1830s, they featured a conservatory, a pond and a menagerie, which was destroyed when a bear escaped. Entrance was free to members of the society; for non-members it cost 1s, except on Saturdays when it cost six pence.

Princess Margaret's Arch

Margaret Tudor, Queen Dowager of Scotland, visited York in 1503 and again in 1516 and 1517, on her way to and from a visit to her brother, Henry VIII. She stayed at St Mary's abbey on both occasions. In 1503, she was met by two sheriffs of York and 100 citizens on horseback, along with the city's great and good. At Micklegate Bar, the mayor, recorder and alderman met her in their finery. The Arch, in the walls opposite Bootham Bar, is named after Margaret, but was built for her father, Henry VII.

The King's Manor

This magnificent, often overlooked, building off Exhibition Square was originally built in 1270 as the house of the Abbott at St Mary's Abbey. It was rebuilt in 1480, the new windows providing the earliest known examples of the use of terracotta as a building material. In 1561, after the Dissolution, the Lord President of the Northern Council took possession. Visitors included Henry VIII and James I; during the Siege of York in 1644, it was the Royalists' headquarters. The ornate doorway with the stunning coat of arms at the main entrance is

Jacobean. The 'IR' stands for James I, who ordered the manor be converted into a royal palace for him to stay in to and from London and Edinburgh. Charles I added the magnificent royal arms, celebrating the Stuarts. After a long period of private lettings and decay, Mr Lumley's Boarding School for Ladies occupied it from 1712–1835, and then the William Wilberforce inspired Yorkshire School for the Blind moved in in 1833. From the 1870s, it was gradually restored and the buildings enlarged, with an added gymnasium and a cloister to create a second courtyard. The Blind School left in 1958; the manor was then acquired by York City Council, who leased it to the University of York in 1963.

Yorkshire School for the Blind

The Wilberforce Memorial was the charity behind the Yorkshire School for the Blind. It was established in the King's Manor on the death of William Wilberforce in 1833, out of a desire to honour his memory and good works in as fitting a manner as possible. Wilberforce had represented Yorkshire as an MP for twenty-eight years and was an influential voice, not just for the movement to abolish the slave trade, but also for the education and training of the blind.

Henry VIII's Hidden Vaults

Under the King's Manor.

Encore!

The encore paradoxically had it's premiere in York, at the Theatre Royal in 1791, after a performance of the *Conjuror's Song* in which a leg of lamb, a cake and a lawyer in a sack were conjured up. The audience enjoyed this so much that they demanded to see it again – a somewhat difficult request to fulfil. Performers and orchestra left the stage amid a salvo of candles and candlesticks; the audience was only placated when the orchestra compromised and returned to play the song again.

Damaged Goods and VD

York Theatre Royal put on *Damaged Goods* in November 1917, promoted as 'The Great Play on the Social Evil ... approved by the highest Ecclesiastical and Medical Authorities.' All profits went to agencies involved in the fight against sexually transmitted infections (or VD in those days).

Blind Tom, *The Inexplicable Phenomenon*

York Theatre Royal was the venue in 1853 for a concert by Miss Greenfield, a black former slave girl; reviews in the *Yorkshire Gazette* were very favourable. In 1866, we heard that 'Blind Tom is Coming! Blind Tom, the Inexplicable Phenomenon', who had recently wowed audiences at the St James's and Egyptian Halls in London (*York Herald,* 20 October). He too was an ex-slave and a protégé of Charles Dickens, who counted him as a 'valued friend'. As a baby Tom was a 'make weight' thrown into the deal when his mother was bought by a tobacco-planter: 'a lump of black flesh born blind, and with the vacant grin of idiocy'. Notwithstanding, he turned out to be a gifted pianist and a success on the novelty and trick circuit. For example, 'his most confusing feat was to play one air with his left hand, another with his right in a different key, whilst he sang a third tune in a different key again...experts such as the Head of Music at Edinburgh testified to his accuracy'.

The York Royal Mint

The first mint in York was set up under the Saxons, producing coins up until the Norman period. The Royal Mint at York was established in St Leonard's in 1279 to relieve the overworked London mint, particularly for the production of farthings. It closed in 1280 and reopened in 1300. Both Edward III and Charles I established Royal Mints in the city.

Tempest Anderson, Volcanologist

Tempest Anderson (1846–1913) was an ophthalmic surgeon at York County Hospital; he was also an expert amateur photographer and volcanologist who witnessed the volcanic eruptions in the West Indies in 1902 and 1907. Born in York, he died on board ship in the Red Sea while returning from a trip to the volcanoes of Indonesia and the Philippines, and is buried in Suez, Egypt. Tempest was President of the York-based Yorkshire Philosophical Society in 1912, when he presented the Society with a 300 seat lecture theatre (the Tempest Anderson Hall) annexed to the Yorkshire Museum. His unrivalled photographic collection exceeds 3,000 images, many of which were taken during his travels.

The Hospitium

People often ask about the purpose of this building. This fine fourteenth-century, half-timbered building in Museum Gardens was probably designed both as a guest house for visitors to the nearby St Mary's Abbey, and as a warehouse for goods for the abbey, unloaded from the river nearby. There was an Elizabethan knot garden with central fountain between the Hospitium and the river.

The Observatory

The observatory was completed in 1833; its 4-inch refractor telescope was built by York's Thomas Cooke in 1850 before he went on to make what was then the largest telescope in the world. York played a crucial role in the development of astronomy in the 1780s when two prominent astronomers – the deaf and dumb John Goodricke (1764–86) and Edward Pigott – laid the foundations of variable star astronomy (the study of stars of varying brightness). Goodricke has a college at the University of York named after him, and Pigott was the first Englishman to discover a comet, which subsequently took his name. The observatory also has a clock from 1811 that tells the time based on the positions of stars. At one time, it was *the* clock by which all others in York were set and is still always four minutes, twenty seconds behind GMT. In the mid-nineteenth century, you had to be a member of the Yorkshire Philosophical Society or it would cost you sixpence to check a timepiece against the observatory clock. The York Observatory originated from a promise made at the very first meeting of the British Association for the Advancement of Science, which took place under the auspices of the Yorkshire Philosophical Society at the Yorkshire Museum in 1831. The vice president of the Royal Astronomical Society, Dr Pearson, promised that if an observatory were built in York, he would personally supply two of his best instruments. He duly obliged, also providing other scientific instruments, including the aforementioned clock. The conical roof was designed by John Smeaton, designer of the Eddystone Lighthouse.

Around the Station

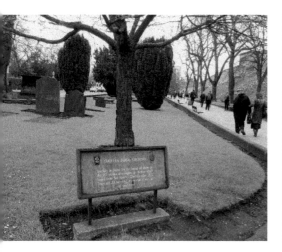

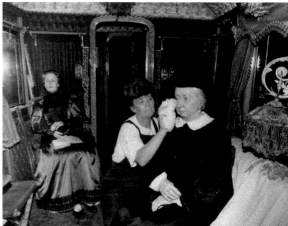

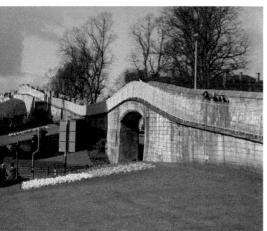

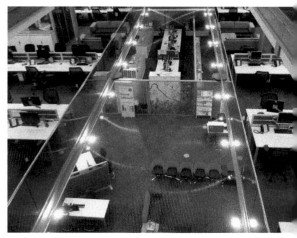

Top left: The cholera burial ground opposite the station and outside the city walls.

Top right: Her Majesty was obviously unamused by something in 1869. Queen Victoria gets a helping hand to wipe away her tears in her saloon coach, now stopped at the National Railway Museum. © York Press

Bottom left: The walls in 2014 – the surrounding gardens are beautifully maintained as ever.

Bottom right: The impressive inside of the council offices converted from York's second railway station and opened for business in 2013.

Cholera – A Disease for the 'Depraved and Immoral'

Cholera probably arrived in York when some 'ragged beggarly gentlefolk' visited the city for the races at the end of May 1832. *The Yorkshire Gazette* identified the first victim as Thomas Hughes, a waterman of 'very irregular habits' who succumbed on 3 June. Hughes had spent the previous week ferrying visitors across the Ouse, many of whom came from cholera-afflicted Selby. *The York Herald* announced it as follows: 'the pestilence of India has (like a thief in the night) silently and unobserved entered our city, and taken up its deadly stands on the vitals of the vitiated, and in the dwellings of the more virtuous poor'. Between this date and mid-September, 185 people died from the disease out of 450 cases (2 per cent of the population); in Yorkshire, only Goole and Hull – both busy ports of course – had higher figures. Looked at another way, the York deaths represented 37 per cent of the deaths expected to be reported in a cholera-free year. Three streets were particularly vulnerable: the Water Lanes with fifteen deaths, Walmgate with twelve and Skeldergate with ten. Hughes' death was not surprising; he lived in Hag Worm Nest, a yard off Skeldergate, which was notoriously filthy according to Laycock in his 'Report on the State of York', with a flooding soil hole and a foul dunghill; indeed, plague had visited Hag Worm Nest in 1551 and in 1604. The fact that the plague started here in 1604 was no coincidence, given the conditions, but the fact that the first case was on 4 June 1604 was eerily coincidental. On 28 June it had spread to the workhouse in Marygate where it killed eight inmates; by 2 July it had reached all parts of the city. By the end, 104 men had died and sixty-nine women, the remainder children.

The 1831 cholera outbreak exemplifies the state of poverty existing in York and the attitudes towards it. Initially, the *Yorkshire Gazette* reported that the disease only affected people 'in want of cleanliness, habits of intemperance and low living, the consequence of poverty and distress'. It described one victim as living in a 'depraved and immoral manner'; another was the wife of a black man, addicted to hard spirits (fourteen glasses a day); another had been drunk for four or five days. Things had changed alarmingly by 9 June when it became obvious that cholera recognised no social or behavioural boundaries. The death of Ruth Bellerby, a Wesleyan Methodist and sister-in-law of the editor of the judgemental *Yorkshire Gazette*, confirmed that beyond all doubt. The cemetery for the victims (all of them) is outside the city walls, opposite the station.

Houses of Correction – Bone Crushing and 'a Terror to Evil-Doers'

There were two in York: one on Old Baile from 1807, the other on Toft Green from 1814. The provision of a treadwheel seems to have exercised the authorities for some time before one was installed in 1825 – 'a terror to evil-doers'. A typical wheel would have been 5 feet in diameter, with twenty-four steps, holding twenty-four convicts taking forty-five steps per minute for ten hours in the summer and seven in winter. The (often disregarded) maximum was limited to 12,000 feet in ascent in one day, or just under 3 miles. Many simply 'ground air', but at Toft Green, the authorities found a commercial angle when they used it in an adjacent bone house for (animal) bone crushing. Unfortunately, the wheel here was also used as a ladder of escape that led to its removal from the wall; it was taken away completely in 1833 and prisoners reverted to smashing boulders.

Botterill's Repository for Horses: 'a Kind of Multi-Storey Horse Car Park'

Built in 1884 next to Lendal Bridge, it was reduced in height by a half in 1965 when it became a car dealers. Patrick Nuttgens described the original building as 'an exotic red and yellow

Byzantine building with ramps inside, up which the horses were led to their stalls – a kind of multi-story horse car park'. It was frequently used by patrons of the 1868 Yorkshire Club for gentlemen (River House) in from the country, just over Lendal Bridge.

Rowntrees, the Donkey and the Parrot

Early days at the Rowntree Tanner's Moat factory were nothing if not lively and exotic; apart from the resident parrot, there was a somewhat temperamental donkey obedient to one man and one man only, and a serious hazard to everyone else. On its dismissal, deliveries were relegated to a handcart. Night-shift workers were sustained by cocoa and pork pies on the firm; most communications to and from Joseph Rowntree were through a trapdoor in the floor of his Lendal Bridge facing office. Hanks the foreman paid the wages each week from a hat full of silver and coppers; each employee would be asked how many hours they had worked and duly paid the going rate from the contents of the hat.

North Eastern Railway Headquarters – a 'Huge Palace of Business'

The building completed in 1906, now a five star hotel, is a magnificent, if extravagant, testament to the power and wealth of the early railways, indeed a 'huge palace of business'. The striking coat of arms includes heraldic elements from the principal cities of those railways, which merged in 1854 to form the NER: York (lions), Leeds (castles), Berwick (bear and oak). Other marvellous features include a gargoyle type figure on the façade and a steam train weathervane.

York's Three Railway Stations

York has had three railway stations. The first was a temporary wooden building on Queen Street outside the walls, opened in 1839 by the York and North Midland Railway. It was replaced in 1841, on Tanner Row within the walls, by what is now called the old York railway station and was built by Robert Stephenson on land owned by Lady Hewley's charity almshouses. Scawin's Railway Hotel opened the same year; it was demolished in 1900. The King of Saxony and Charles Dickens were amongst travellers arriving here. The buildings were reminiscent of Euston Station in Euston Square. Access was difficult from North Street, and this eventually led to the construction of Hudson Street (after George Hudson), and Lendal Bridge. Because through trains between London and Newcastle needed to reverse out of George Hudson's old York station in order to continue their journey, a new station was built outside the walls. This is the present station, designed by the North Eastern Railway architects Thomas Prosser and William Peachey, which opened in 1877. It had thirteen platforms and was at that time the largest station in the world. At 800 feet long and 234 feet wide, this is one of the most spectacular examples of railway architecture in the world, rightly and famously described as 'A splendid monument of extravagance', and 'York's propylaeum'. As part of the new station project, the Royal Station Hotel (now The Royal York Hotel), designed by Peachey, opened in 1878.

Micklegate & Bishophill

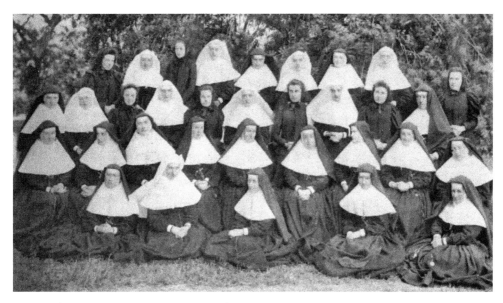

Above: The Bar Convent community around 1900.

Below: The Bar Convent today.

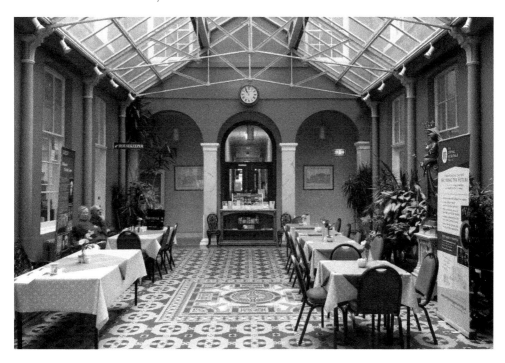

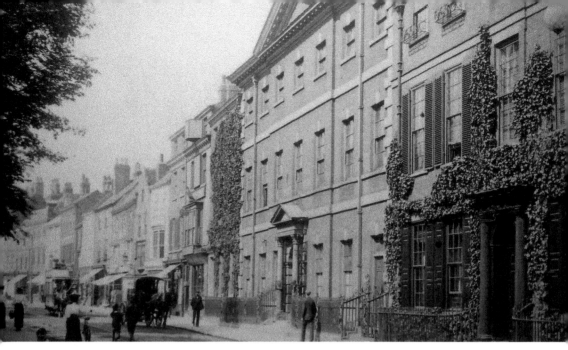

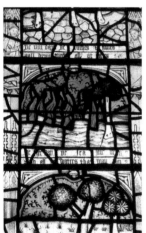

Above: Micklegate and its fine houses around 1910.

Left: A detail from the breathtaking *Pricke of Conscience* window from 1410 in All Saints, North Street. The detail shows (from top) rocks and stones consumed by fire, the sea catching fire and the sea receding, exposing the sea bed.

Below: Happy girls from St Stephen's Orphanage, Trinity Street, York on a day trip to Filey in July 1919. The orphanage was founded in the 1870s, originally in Precentor's Court, moving to Trinity Lane and then to the Mount in 1919. It closed in 1969. Its aim was to accommodate and educate poor girls who had lost one or both parents. The image is part of the Evelyn Collection. © YAYAS

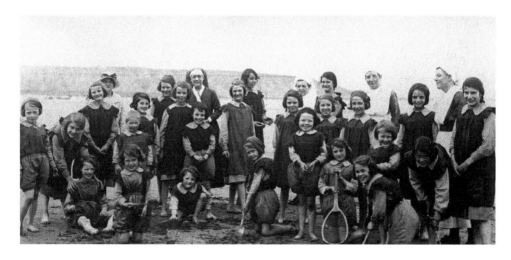

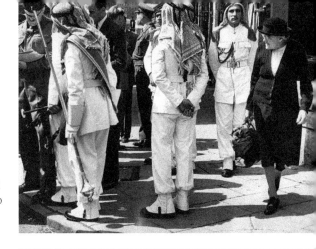

The Arab Legion comes to York in 1955 for the Northern Command Tattoo – what the old lady thought of it is anyone's guess. The tattoo was held at the Knavesmire, this was shot at Micklegate Bar. © York Press

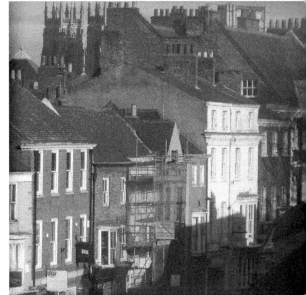

Micklegate from the bar.

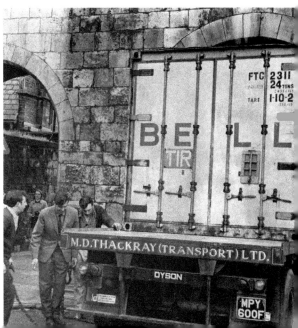

This 20-foot fertiliser truck was stuck in Micklegate Bar for three hours in October 1969. A spokesman for the council said, 'I wouldn't mind if this driver was a foreigner but he only comes from Malton'. © York Press

The Clandestine Bar Convent

The first mass was held in April 1769 in the new chapel, with its magnificent, but externally unobtrusive, neoclassical dome concealed beneath a pitched slate roof. Apart from the discreet dome, the building has many other integral features, which betray the secret nature of its activities. The chapel is situated in the centre of the building so that it cannot be seen from the street; its plain windows reveal nothing of its ecclesiastical nature and there are no fewer than eight exits, providing escape routes for the congregation in the event of a religious raid. There is also a priest's hole that can still be seen today. The nuns who still live there belong to the Congregation of Jesus, which was founded by Mary Ward (1585–1645). Five nuns were tragically killed here during the 1942 Baedecker air raid.

Mary Ward

Mary Ward (d. 1645) is celebrated in the museum that is an integral part of the Bar Convent. She is buried in St Thomas's in Osbaldwick. She founded the Institute of the Blessed Virgin Mary opening schools in Flanders before the order was suppressed by the Pope. After imprisonment in Munich for heresy, she returned to England and re-established the institute in Heworth in 1644. The fifty pictures on the Bar Convent staircase depict her life; they are reproduced from seventeenth century paintings from the house of the Institute of Augsburg. The 2,000 or so books in the library date from between 1508 and 1850 and, unlike some library collections, are well used, read and annotated. The convent also retains a relic of the hand of St Margaret Clitherow.

Sister Mary Xaveria

Born in 1784, Sister Mary was a nun and a teacher at the Bar Convent and became headmistress at the Poor School there in 1830. An earlier appointment was at St George's School in Walmgate, where she taught 'a disorderly crowd of wild looking little creatures for the most part barefooted, squalid and dirty, shouting and screaming'. Her solution was, in uncanny anticipation of Sister Maria in *The Sound of Music,* to sing, and her voice 'acted like magic on the undisciplined audience. In a few moments they were standing silent and almost motionless'.

The Refuge, 'For Such Miserable Young Females'

Many York prostitutes found scanty reward in their non-industrial city and turned for support to the Penitentiary Society (the Refuge), established in 1822 in Bishophill to rescue and rehabilitate girls in prostitution. The Refuge was set up in 1845 as a 'place of permanent refuge for such miserable young females as may seem in the spirit of true penitence'. The aim was to help them reform over a two-year period and to allow them escape from the brothels, many of which were clustered around the minster, and Friargate, close to the Castlegate Meeting House, spreading south through the city. There are records of 1,400 prostitutes and brothel keepers in the city between 1837 and 1887; of the 412 girls admitted to the Refuge between 1845 and 1887, only 142 were rehabilitated and found work in service, although many of these too returned to their former ways.

Victoria Bar

This bar was built in 1838 and named after the new Queen. It gave access to the city in the Nunnery Lane area. During construction, an earlier archway was uncovered, which showed signs of having been hastily blocked up. This was probably the twelfth-century bar known as Lounelith, or 'secluded gate'; the blockade was possibly part of the strengthening of the city's defences in the Northern Rebellion in 1569.

Micklegate Bar – 'Off with his Head and Set it on York's Gates; so York did Overlook the Town of York'

Micklegate Bar was originally called Mickleith, which means great gate. The royal arms are those of Edward III; the arch is Norman, the rest fourteenth century, the side arch was added in 1753. Being on the road to and from London, this was the bar through which royal visitors entered York. Edward IV, Richard III, Henry VII, Margaret Tudor, James I, Charles I (on three Civil War occasions) and James II all passed through. Henry VIII was scheduled to enter here but, in the event, came in through Walmgate Bar. Heads and quarters of traitors were routinely displayed on the top, most famously Lord Scrope of Mastan in 1415; Sir Henry Percy (Hotspur) after his part in the rebellion against Elizabeth I; Richard Duke of York after the Battle of Wakefield in 1460, prompting Shakespeare to write 'Off with his head and set it on York's gates; so York did overlook the town of York' (Queen Margaret, *Henry VI*); Thomas Percy in 1569 – his head remained there for two years. Removal of heads without permission was, appropriately, punishable by beheading – guess where the heads ended up? The last displays were in 1746 after the Jacobite Rebellion at Culloden. The heads of James Mayne and William Connelly remained on the bar until 1754. The barbican was removed in 1826 to allow a circus access to the city; the east side arch was built in 1827.

Jacob's Well

An often overlooked fifteenth-century timber-framed house in Trinity Lane off Micklegate; it became an inn from 1750 to 1903 called The Jacob's Well. The unusual fifteenth-century canopy over the door was taken from The Wheatsheaf in Davygate, at one time the residence of the Bishops of Durham.

The Temporary House for the Friendless and Fallen

At No. 7 Trinity Lane around 1816.

The Buttermarket

York's main trade in the eighteenth century was butter – the market was in St Martin's churchyard with its seventeenth-century butter stand. Dairymaids each milked nine cows for £9 per year.

The Hainault Riots

In 1327, 60,000 or so troops were stationed in Walmgate with Edward II in preparation for war against the Scots. The garrison included allied troops from Hainault and Zeeland, many of whom were slain by the English when skirmishes broke out after a banquet held by the king at the castle. 300 soldiers in the army of Sir John Beaumont and eighty Lincolnshire archers were killed and buried in a mass grave in St Clement's church graveyard in Fossgate. Hostilities resumed in 1329 during the festivities for the marriage of Edward III and Philippa of Hainault in York; 242 English and 347 Hainaulters died on the banks of the Ouse.

All Saints, North Street and the Fourteenth-Century Man with Glasses

The striking spire is the least of this church's many treasures. Emma Raughton, a visionary anchorite, lived in an anchorhold here – a two-storey house attached to the aisle. Other marvels include a figure in one of the fourteenth-century windows wearing glasses – one of the earliest depictions of spectacles – and representations of the green man in the aisles and nave.

Our Ladye of the Rosary – Your Last Fifteen Days on this Earth

The church has some of the finest medieval stained glass in Europe that is *not* actually in York Minster, including the aisle window, which shows the Six Corporal Acts of Mercy (as in Matthew) and the famous 1410 Doom Window (or 'Pricke of Conscience' window), which graphically depicts your final fifteen days on this earth before the Day of Judgement. Panels include such cataclysms as the stars falling from heaven; earthquakes and a church spire (All Saints'?) crashing to the ground; fishes and sea monsters rising from the seas; a skeleton representing Death stalking the Earth; three coffins full of bones appearing; people hiding in holes and everything and everyone being consumed by fire.

Kidcotes Prison

A prison, long gone, on the Old Ouse Bridge. By the end of the fourteenth century, York had seven prisons, each incarcerating different kinds of criminal. The Sheriff of York and the mayor each had their own prisons on either side of the old Ouse Bridge. Prisoners could languish for up to ten years waiting for trial, during which time they had to pay rent and board. Running a prison could be a profitable business. York had the only dedicated 'forest prison' for locking up criminals who had broken the laws of the forest of Galtres. It was on Davygate in Davy Hall.

Ouse Bridge

The bridge itself was a self-contained community of its own. Rather like the Ponte Vecchio in Florence, it was home to a number of facilities and buildings. It had a council chamber, St William's chapel, two prisons (Kidcotes and a debtors') and Agnes Grethede, who, around 1544, was paid 2s a year to clean the 'pyssing howes on Ouse Bridge'.

Cooke, Troughton and Simms – Optical Instrument Manufacturers

In 1856, Cooke moved into the Buckingham Works built on the site of the home of the second Duke of Buckingham at Bishophill – one of Britain's first purpose-built telescope factories. He built a telescope for Prince Albert in 1860 and one for a Gateshead millionaire: the telescope tube was 32 feet long and the whole instrument weighed 9 tons – the biggest telescope in the world at the time. In 1893, H. D. Taylor, optical manager, designed the Cooke Photographic Lens, which became the basic design for most camera lenses thereafter. In 1866, Thomas Cooke branched out into three-wheeled steam cars, which reached the dizzy speed of 15 mph. They, were, however, outlawed by the Road Act, which prohibited vehicles which travelling in excess of 4 mph. In those days, a man with a red flag had to walk in front of any vehicle not pulled by a horse. Cooke fitted his steam engine into a boat and travelled on the Ouse, free of horses and red flags. He died in 1868.

Friends' Burial Ground, Bishophill

In keeping with Quaker practice, the graves here are all very simple and describe only the age of the deceased and the date of death, so as not 'to exalt the creature'. Months are given in numerals only; there are two reasons for this: firstly, the names we use celebrate pagan gods and, secondly, where this is not the case, they are sometimes wrong, as in the case of December, which is not our tenth month. Notable denizens include Lindley Murray (d.1726) and William Tuke. Murray was author of *The English Grammar*, published in 1795 for staff and pupils of the Girl's Friend's School (later the Mount). The book went into 170 editions, the last of which was published in the USA in 1871. A new Quaker burial ground opened in Heslington Road in 1855.

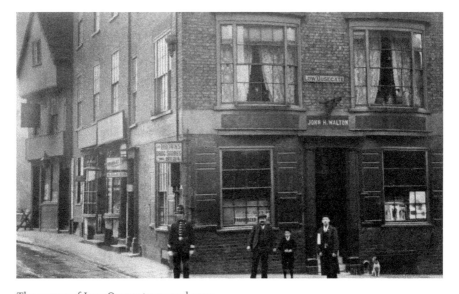

The corner of Low Ousegate around 1900.

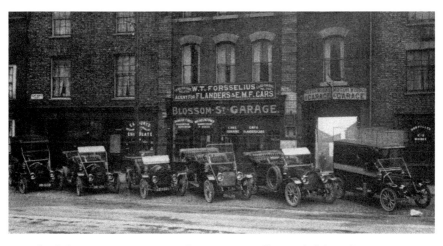

Forsselius' Blossom Street Garage in the 1920s. Forssellius traded there from 1908 to 1922.

The Castle Area

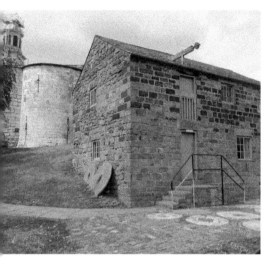
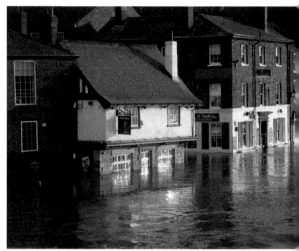

Above left: Raindale Mill: Mill on the Foss behind the castle.

Above right: The King's Arms: the pub that is never dry. Some fairly usual flooding on King's Staithe, New Year's Day 2013.

Below: Now known as Fishergate Bar, gateway to Selby. The John Smith's Phoenix Inn brewery can be seen to the right in Long Close Lane. The building on the left was Falconer's the furnishers. St George's Roman Catholic church can be seen in the distance, built in 1850 to meet the spiritual demands of Irish immigrants.

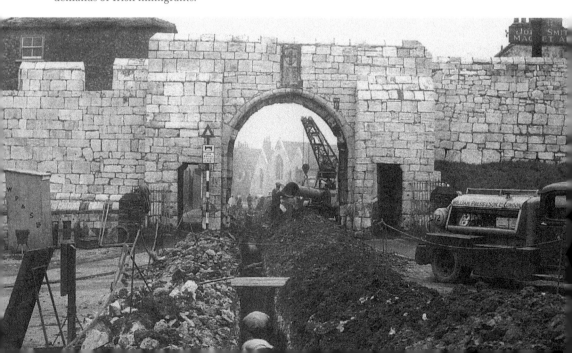

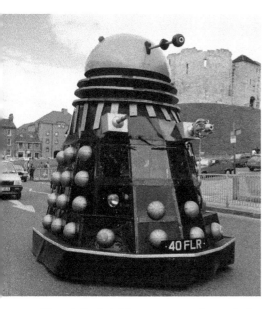
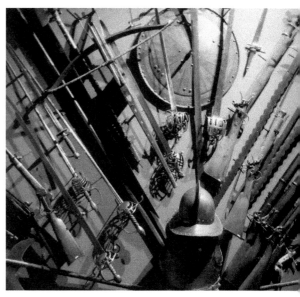

Above left: A dalek sweeps past the castle in 1990. It came from the nearby Museum of Automata, now sadly exterminated, and was nine feet high, built on a Mini 1100 chassis. © York Press

Above right: A selection of arms and armour in York Castle Museum.

Below: Taken from a postcard franked in 1911, this is tobacco advertising for WD&HO Wills in an unashamed exploitation of children. The location is St George's Field during Hospital Saturday.

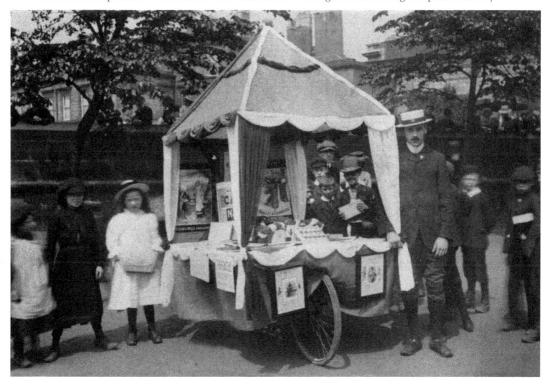

Clifford's Tower and the Jewish Massacre

Originally King's Tower, or even the Minced Pie, but from 1596, named after Francis Clifford, Earl of Cumberland, who restored it for use as a garrison after it had been partly dismantled by Robert Redhead in 1592. An alternative etymology comes from Roger de Clifford, whose corpse was hung there in chains in 1322. Built in wood by William the Conqueror – his first English castle – when he visited to establish his northern headquarters in 1190, it was burnt down when 150 terrified York Jews sought sanctuary here from an anti-semitic mob. Faced with the choice of being killed or forced baptism, many committed suicide, 150 others were slaughtered. It was rebuilt in stone by King John and Henry III as a quadrilobate between 1245 and 1259, as a self-contained stronghold and royal residence; it housed the kingdom's treasury in the fourteenth century. Robert Aske, one of the prime movers in the Pilgrimage of Grace, was hanged here on 12 July 1537. Deer grazed around the tower for many years. It became part of the prison in 1825.

Water Lane War Crime

Another little-known York atrocity. Duke 'Butcher' Cumberland, on his victorious return from bloody Culloden, left a number of prisoners here to show his gratitude for the city's hospitality. The Sheriff's chaplain read out the message: 'And the Lord said unto Moses "Take all the heads of the people and hang them up before the sun"'. Twenty-three were duly left to hang for ten minutes, stripped and quartered, their heads stuck on Micklegate Bar. Water Lane was renamed Cumberland Street in celebration of the butcher Duke.

Fulford Biscuits

World famous Fulford Biscuits in Coppergate and Heslington Road was run by Miss A. and Miss F. Challenger. They had brought their confectionery skills from Sheffield and Harrogate, and bought the sole rights to produce the famous, secret recipe for Fulford Biscuits, from the estate of the late Mrs G. Leng. The Leng business had been set up in the 1820s and won prizes at the Leeds Exhibition in 1868 and the York Exhibition in 1866. In her *Good Things in England* (1932), Florence White says that they 'tasted like a mixture of a Bath Oliver and plain water biscuit ... and they were delicious'.

Baile Hill – York's Other Castle

The first of York's two castles built by William the Conqueror in 1068 and fortified with a timber fort; it soon became redundant.

Bitch Daughter Tower

On Baile Hill it has in its time been pressed into service as the King's prison until 1868, a Civil War guardhouse and gun emplacement and as a cowshed. It was originally three storeys high but the upper rooms were quarried to repair Ouse Bridge in 1567. Early names include 'Biche Doughter' in 1566 and `le bydoutre' in 1451.

Mutton Curry, Gin-soaked Hangman

In 1802, William Curry (or Curry Wilkinson, or Thomas Askern) was sentenced to death for sheep stealing (for which he earned the nickname Mutton Curry) and was destined for the long drop at the Knavesmire. Fortunately, a hangman was needed at the castle and Curry was offered the job.

By 1810, he had performed twenty-five executions. All did not always go well though. In 1821, he reported to the scaffold somewhat drunk and unable to find the doomed William Brown's neck; he was beaten up on his way home for his ineptitude. Later that year he was about to hang five prisoners when he, again worse the wear from drink, fell down the drop with the convicts. He retired, twenty hangings later, *otium sine dignitate* ('retirement without dignity') to the Thirsk Poor House in 1835. *The Yorkshire Gazette* pointed out that 'gin was apt to provide a snare for him'.

Wiggington Roads – A Fine Day Out for 5,000

In 1868, the New Drop replaced the public gallows, which had moved from the Knavesmire in 1801. It was situated where the roundabout at St George's car park is today. Roughly opposite in the Castle Museum wall is a small doorway, through which the condemned were led to the gallows. The last public execution was of Frederick Parker in 1868, a convicted murderer; 5,000 people came to gawp. After that, hangings were behind closed doors at the New Drop. The last man to hang in York under the black flag was August Carlsen, who was hanged at the New Drop on 29 February 1896 for the murder of Julia Wood. Other gallows existed in Burton Stone Lane controlled by the abbot of St Mary's abbey and at the Horse Fair, at the junction of the Haxby and Wiggington Roads. There were gallows on Foss Bridge administered by the Archbishop of York. Those owned by St Leonard's church were on Green Dykes, now Garrow Hill and close to Thief Lane, along which convicted robbers were led to the scaffold.

Dick Turpin 'Expir'd in Five Minutes'

Highwayman Dick Turpin, also known as John Palmer, was hanged (somewhat fittingly) on the Knavesmire in 1739, for horse stealing – 'a crime worthy of death'. Turpin spent his last six months in the Debtors' Prison, which was built in 1701–05 and is now part of the Castle Museum; the other half of the museum was originally the Female Prison, built in 1780–83. The museum, which opened in 1938, is named after York Castle, part of which originally stood on the site. Turpin had many visitors. His jailer is said to have earned £100 from selling drinks to Turpin and his guests; Turpin bought a new frock coat and shoes and hired five mourners for £3 10s for the occasion. A report in *The Gentleman's Magazine* for 7 April 1739 notes Turpin's arrogance: 'Turpin behaved in an undaunted manner; as he mounted the ladder, feeling his right leg tremble, he spoke a few words to the topsman, then threw himself off, and expir'd in five minutes.' The short drop method of hanging meant that those executed were killed by slow strangulation: Turpin was left hanging until late afternoon, before being cut down and taken to *The Blue Boar Inn* in Castlegate. Turpin's grave in St George's churchyard was dug particularly deep to deter body snatchers; to no avail: the corpse was removed and found later at the back of Stonegate in a surgeon's garden. Before reburial the coffin was filled with

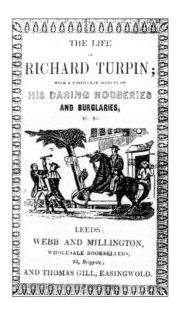

An advertisement for a novel based on the exploits of Dick Turpin, published in Easingwold.

lime. Black Bess, Turpin's steed, was an elaboration added later by writers such as William Harrison Ainsworth in *Rockwood* (1878) and Eliza Cook in her *Black Bess* (1869), an interesting line from which reads: 'And the fame of Dick Turpin had been something less If he'd ne'er rode to York on his bonnie Black Bess'.

Raindale Mill – Mill on the Foss

An early nineteenth-century flour mill removed from Raindale, Newton on the North York Moors to the grounds of the York Castle Museum in the 1965, close to the River Foss.

St George's Super Cinema

Opened in 1921 as an annexe to Fairfax House, it could seat 1,340 viewers, including 450 in the balcony. The screen was 22 feet by 18 and the orchestra was led by Harold Croke. The first film was *Three Men in a Boat*; seat prices ranged from 8*d* to 1*s* 6*d*.

Fulford Open-Air School

Originally opened at No. 11 Castlegate in 1913, in the same building as the Tuberculosis Dispensary, it moved in 1914 to a converted army hut in the grounds of Fulford House. It then became known as Fulford Road School for Delicate and Partially Sighted Children. The open-air school movement was set up in 1904 in Berlin to curb the development of tuberculosis in children and, as such, required the establishment of schools that combined medical care with teaching adapted to pupils with pre-tuberculosis. Fulford closed in 1960 and was demolished in 1964. The Holgate Bridge School for Mentally Defective Boys was opened in 1911 and moved to Fulford House, later known as Fulford Road School for Educationally Sub-Normal Children, in 1923.

The Phoenix and the Black Babies

In George Street near Fishergate Bar, the original name until the mid-1800s was The Labour in Vain. The sign depicted a white woman scrubbing a black baby to make it white, in vain. The more prosaic new name derives from the Phoenix Iron Foundry, which stood nearby. The Bar had been walled up in 1489 as punishment for the locals who had rioted against a tax levied to pay for a war against Brittany; it was reopened to provide access to the new cattle market in 1827.

Oliver's Army

The remains of 113 Cromwellian soldiers were found under where All Saint's church stood in Fishergate in 2007. In the ten mass graves, the soldiers were packed liked sardines, face down or on their sides – no buckles, buttons or jewellery was found with them. The likelihood is that they all died from a particularly virulent disease soon after their victory at Marston Moor.

Zotofoam Baths and 'Wanted Secretions'

These foam and tonic baths were installed at St George's Baths Building in 1935; they were reputed to be effective against rheumatism and obesity. Cost was 2*s* 6*d* for twenty minutes. Hot air is forced into a hot bath followed by a squeeze of Zotofoam, providing a body massasge to 'eliminate unwanted secretions from the pores of the skin'. Dubbed as a jacuzzi on steroids, they were popular until the 1960s.

Shambles & Fossgate, Peasholme Green, Foss Islands

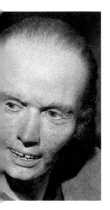 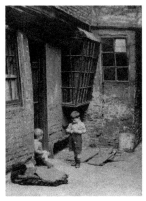 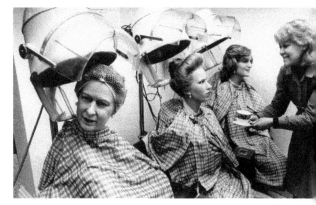

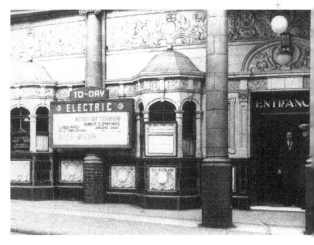

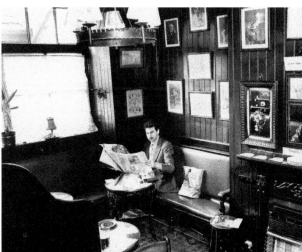

Above left: Meet Eymund. He was part of the AD 975 Jorvik Cityscape, and is a reconstruction from a Viking skeleton found in Fishergate. © York Press

Above middle: Pump Court and the unforgivably neglected lantern tower window in the 1950s. © York Press

Above right: Hair stylist Janet Brown attends to some posh visitors in 1984. The Princess Royal looks less than impressed with her cup of tea. The models were on a day out from the Friargate Wax Museum. © York Press

Middle right: The Electric Cinema in Fossgate, 1949. This was York's first purpose-built cinema, opened in 1911. It survives as a furniture store. © York Press

Bottom right: The all too comfortable back room in The Blue Bell, Fossgate, in 1985. © York Press

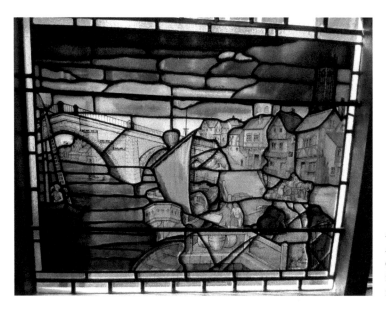

A window in the Merchant Adventurer's Hall depicting York trade and industry from the late nineteenth century.

Crafts and Trades in York

Butchers were famously focused in Shambles. Less well-known, Ousegate and Castlegate were the haunt of lorimers (makers of bits and bridles) and spurriers; cutlers were to be found near St Michael-le-Belfry; pinners at St Crux; girdlers at Girdlergate (Church Street); tanners near North Street (hence Tanner's Moat and Tanner Row); fishmongers on the Foss and Ouse Bridges; parchment workers, leather workers and prostitutes at Harlot Hill (St Maurice's Road today), and harlots fittingly also in Grope (Grape) Lane.

Pump Court and the Hidden Lantern Tower Window

At the junction of King's Court and Newgate, Pump Court was the site of one of the many water pumps and wells that served the city. Piped water was turned on in parts of the city between 1677 and 1685 and a public bathhouse opened in 1691. John Wesley preached in a room (the Oven) here in 1753 (one of twenty-six visits to the city); it became an official place of worship for Methodists in 1754. One of the country's only two surviving lantern tower windows in Britain is in Pump Court, tragically and negligently, almost hidden from public view. Betty Petre lived here; she kept her cattle in the court before slaughter in Shambles. Mr Huber collected sheeps' guts and washed them in a drain before exporting them to Germany to make fiddle strings. Other residents included a chimney sweep and a prostitute, referred to locally as 'an old knock'.

The Margaret Clitherow Oratory

Mulier fortis – brave woman. The wife of John Clitherow, a butcher who lived here at No. 35 (or possibly at No. 10), they were married in St Martin-le-Grand in Coney Street. The house became a refuge for priests on the run. Margaret first saw the inside of a jail in 1577 (the Castle Prison) for nine months for not attending church. She was jailed twice more at York Castle (1580 for six months and 1583 for eighteen months). Between 1582 and 1583, five priests were executed at Tyburn, and Margaret would go at night to the gallows to conduct a vigil over the bodies.

She was found guilty in 1586 of 'harbouring and maintaining Jesuits and seminary priests, traitors to Her Majesty'. She had been given away by a Flemish boy in her care who had been threatened with a naked beating if he did not reveal the priest holes. The usual penalty was hanging, but, because she refused to offer a plea ('having made no offence, I need no trial'), Margaret was sentenced to death by having a door weighted with nearly half a ton of boulders placed on top of her. The execution took place at the tollbooth on Ouse Bridge. Within fifteen minutes, she was dead; her ribcage had collapsed and burst through her skin. Her body was dumped but found later, apparently with no signs of decay. Margaret was beatified in 1929 and canonised in 1970 by Pope Paul VI who described her as the 'Pearl of York'. Her embalmed hand is in the Bar Convent. A church in Haxby is dedicated to her.

The Electric Theatre, Fossgate – a 'Laugh and Scratch'
One of six cinemas in York in 1929. It was opened in 1911; the entrance was through a door beneath the screen. From 1951 it was known as the Scala. It closed in 1957 and became a furniture shop. The exterior is still beautifully preserved today. Locally, it was known as the Flea Bin, and a visit meant a 'laugh and scratch'. Admission on Saturday afternoon was 4d or a clean jam jar (an early example of recycling).

The Blue Bell
This, York's smallest pub and one of the best, is in Fossgate. It was built in 1798 when the back of the pub faced on to Fossgate and the front was in Lady Peckett's Yard. The Rowntrees were responsible for turning it around in 1903, no doubt because one of their temperance preaching adult schools was in Lady Peckett's Yard. York City FC held their board meetings here, and in The Second World War it served as a soup kitchen. Women were barred from the public bar until the 1990s.

York Confectionery Co. – Puffy's
A little known York confectionery company. Founded in 1867 in Fossgate, then moving to Fenwick Street off Bishopthorpe Road, it specialised in candied peel and red-and-white mint rock for the seaside market. York Confectionery Co. was owned by a man called Henderson; little is known about him apart from that he suffered from dyspnea, shortness of breath, and his factory became known as Puffy's as a result. He went bankrupt in 1909.

Kidnapping Carmelites
The Carmelites were established in their friary by about 1400, on land between Fossgate and Hungate. In 1358, a certain Richard Thornton was 'within the years of puberty [he] was lately ensnared and seduced by the Carmelites ... and took the habit'. The young victim was under fourteen years of age at the time; the incident caused such outrage that Edward III took the boy 'into his protection and his special defence'. In 1374, a friar called John Wy killed his colleague, John Harald. Wy was pardoned and exonerated. To put this cover-up into context, the friary 'plastrer', John de Driffield, was fined twenty marks for 'building an oven ... so badly that it utterly collapsed'.

The Roman Amphitheatre
There is no doubt that Roman York boasted an amphitheatre; the only mystery surrounds the exact location. It now seems credible that it was located in the St Saviourgate area. Street names

such as Stonebow (stone arch) and Aldwark (old works) are sympathetic to the existence of an arched building, while Aldwark itself and Hungate both curve – possibly around the walls of the amphitheatre.

The Walker Iron Foundry – 'Ironfounders and Purveyors of Smithy Work to the Queen'

One of York's lesser-known industrial successes. Founded in 1837 by John Walker (1801–53), 'Iron and brass founder, bell-hanger and smith', in Dixon's Yard, Walmgate. They provided the first gas lamps and railings for St Leonards Place, the gates at Dean's Park and the surrounding railings and gas lights. In 1845/46, Walker supplied the gates to Kew Gardens, a commission that earned them the patronage of Queen Victoria in 1847 when she granted them permission to describe themselves as 'Ironfounders and Purveyors of Smithy Work to the Queen'. In 1853, they supplied the 10-ton gates and railings to the British Museum, London. Other commissions included gates at Sandringham, the Botanical Gardens in Mauritius and the palace of the Maharajah Holkar of India. Renamed Thomlinson-Walker, the firm moved to the Victoria Foundry at No. 76 Walmgate.

Walmgate Bar

The only bar to retain its barbican – until 1959, a family lived in there. In 1570, the bar was guarded 'so that no suspect person of Rotherham or Selby resort unto this city'.

The Black Swan – Cock Fights and General Wolfe of Quebec

The Black Swan in Peasholme Green, a former coaching station, is seriously haunted. Also known as The Mucky Duck, it is one of the oldest licensed houses in York. Originally, it was the home of William Bowes, former sheriff, mayor and MP between 1417 and 1428. It still has a fine oak staircase and a magnificent Delft fireplace. The upstairs room was used for illegal cockfights; the grill used by the guard to watch the stairs can still be seen. Gen. Wolfe's family lived here; it was the HQ of the York Layerthorpe Cycling Club from 1834. The Leeds Arms (closed 1935) was next door on the corner of Haymarket and the Woolpack was over the road.

The King's Fishpool – 'the Disgrace of York ... a Stinking Morass'

Stagnating around the Red Tower, created when the Normans dammed the River Foss. It was variously described as 'the disgrace of York ... a stinking morass' and by Francis Drake as the repository for 'any dung of beasts or other nastinesses'. The Corporation drained it in 1854 and built Foss Islands Road.

The Red Tower – Gunpowder Warehouse

The Red Tower (named after the colour of its brickwork – all the other walls, bars and towers being built with Tadcaster limestone) is just off Foss Islands Road. Its walls are 4 feet thick. The tower was built around 1490 by Henry VII and restored in 1857, after being damaged in the Civil War siege of York. The original roof was flat and boasted a projecting toilet. It was also known as Brimstone House when it was used as a gunpowder warehouse; around 1800 it was a stables.

Further Afield

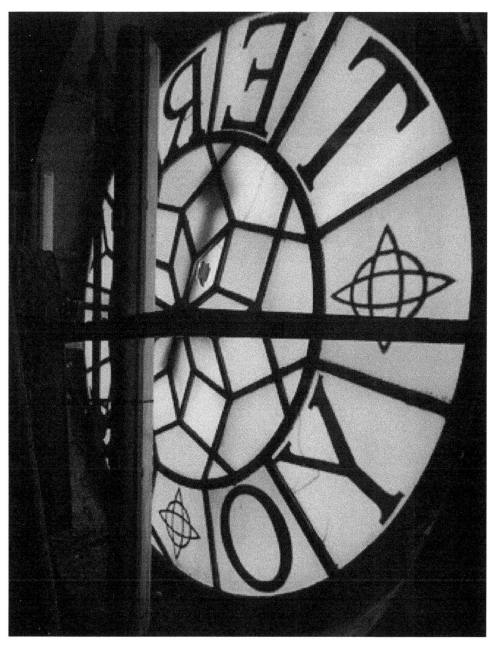

Terry's clock face from the inside, during redevelopment of the building. Courtesy of Tassadar@ midlandsheritageforum.co.uk.

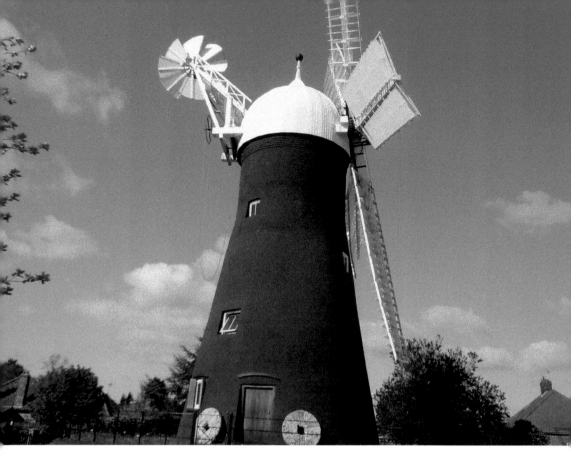

Above: The 1770 windmill in Holgate after the recent reconstruction.

Below: Visitor parking at the 1903 Ebor Meeting at the Knavesmire. © York Press

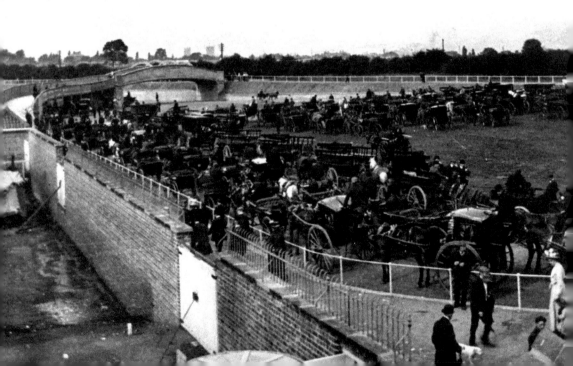

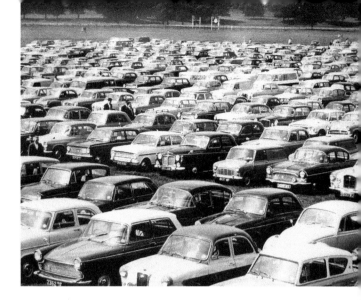

Visitor parking at the 1965 Ebor
Meeting at the Knavesmire.

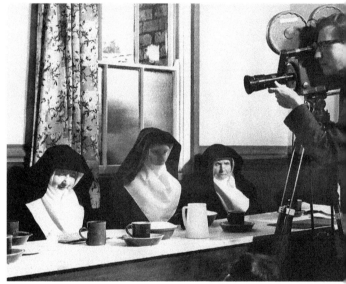

Camera-shy Poor Clares.
© York Press

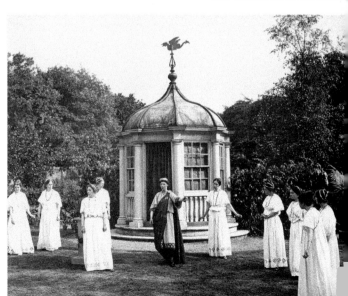

A Greek tragedy in mid-performance
by girls of the Mount School.

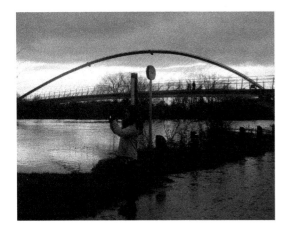
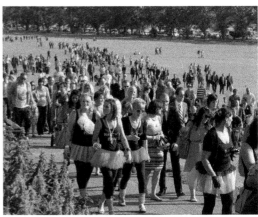

Above left: The Millennium Bridge, Christmas 2013. The photographer is Rachael Chrystal.

Above right: Leaving the Knavesmire for a night on the city after the 2012 Ebor Meeting.

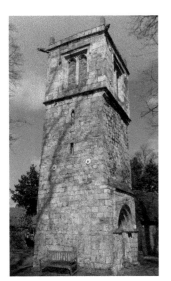
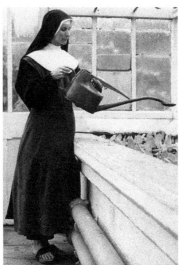
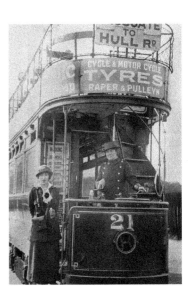

Above left: The neglected Norman tower from the original church in the grounds of St. Lawrence's and St. Hilda's church in Lawrence Street. The original church had its fifteen minutes of fame when architect John Vanbrugh was married here in 1719.

Above middle: Self-sufficiency at the Poor Clares in the 1970s. © York Press

Above right: Taken during the First World War when many men were away at the front; women replaced the men, but had usually lost their jobs to returning servicemen by 1920. This is car 21, stopped at the Hull Road terminus at the Beeswing Hotel. The extra disk in the headlamp was to diffuse the light during air raids; the 'H' indicated the Hull Road route. The photograph is in the collection of Roy Barrell and was originally published in Old Glory #117, November 1999.

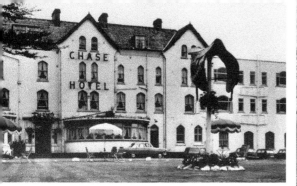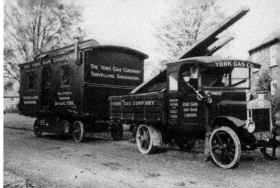

Above left: The Chase Hotel (now the Marriott) in the 1960s; note the huge saddle in the front garden.

Above right: A mobile gas shop in 1929. © York Press

The Poor Clares

The forty nuns came to York from Bruges. The first convent of the Sisters of the Second Order of Saint Francis was Plantation House in Hull Road in 1865; they moved to the obscure St Joseph's Monastery in Lawrence Street in 1873. Until recently, they lived there behind 20-ft high walls, got up at 5.00 a.m., lived in silence, were vegetarians and cultivated a 6-acre garden to make themselves largely self-sufficient. The convent comprised cloisters, cells, chapel and refrectory. The remaining eight Poor Clare Colettines have now moved to Askham Bryan. The convent's Mother Abbess sought permission from the Vatican for the move and admitted to mixed feelings: 'it's only bricks and mortar', she said.

The Cold War Bunker

York's worst kept secret. Opened, or rather closed, in 1961, this piece of Cold War furniture was officially No. 20 Group Royal Observer HQ operated by UKWMO, the UK Warning and Monitoring Organisation. Its role was to function as one of twenty-nine monitoring and listening posts in the event of a nuclear explosion. Decommissioned in 1991, English Heritage have opened it to the public to enable them to see the decontamination areas, living quarters, communications centre and operations rooms.

Holgate Mill

The majestic 1770 five-sail mill built on the site of a fifteenth-century predecessor. At that time, Holgate was a village with a population of fifty-five souls. Unusually, the mill had five double-shuttered sails; they were damaged in a 1930 storm and taken down, after which time the mill was powered by an electric motor. The Holgate Windmill Preservation Society looks after the mill today and completed a marvellous reconstruction in 2012.

The Chase Hotel – 'Gateway to York'

Now the Marriott (since 2001) in Tadcaster Road, the Chase was part of the deal relating to the construction of York's present railway station. Their Yorkshire and North Midland Railway house, occupied by the Close Family, near to the cholera burial ground was in the way of the new development. To tempt the Close family to leave, the North Eastern Railway agreed to build them a new house in 1876. It became Harkers Hotel in 1927 (which had moved from St Helen's Square), before being renamed the Chase Hotel in 1948. A huge saddle decorated the forecourt for many years.

Cats, Ghosts, Plague, Drownings, Child Abuse & World Wars

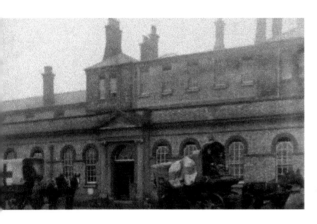

Fulford Military Hospital with ambulances. It was built in 1862 by the War Department, with extensions in 1879, 1914 and during the Second World War.

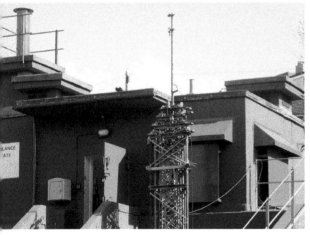

York's very own Cold War nuclear shelter. Now a tourist attraction.

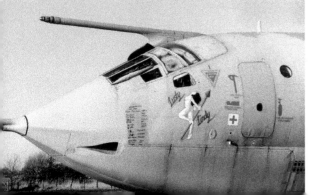

Lusty Lindy: a Nimrod which was converted to a mid-air re-fuelling aircraft in its later years. Photographed here at the Elvington Air Museum in 1995.
© York Press

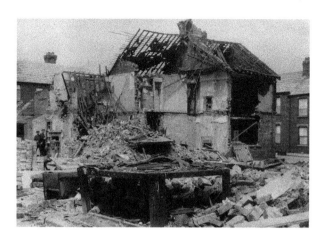

Bombed houses after an air raid in 1942. © York Press

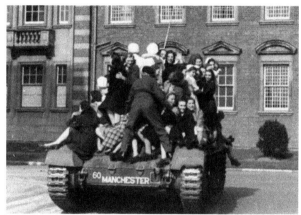

A Second World War fundraising tank at Terry's.

York's Cats

The hallmark of Tom Adams, the York architect who died in 2006. Cats prowl, or have prowled, on buildings in Bedern, St Andrewgate (two) King's Square (with pigeon), Colliergate (two); one past the Quilting Museum, Goodramgate, Gillygate, Museum Gardens entrance, Coney Street, Ousegate (two); one opposite the Park Inn; two at the junction of Friars Terrace and South Esplanade on King's Staith; Shambles and Walmgate. All show Adams' work to be reminiscent of Leonardo da Vinci (who made use of a cat) rather than Robert Thompson of Kilburn (who used a mouse). There are around twenty-three in all (or there were – some have been catnapped).

Plague

In the Plague of 1604, all dogs and cats were put down; the exterminating officer was paid 2d for every cat slain and was allowed to keep the skins. In 1631, a citizen called Luke received a public flogging for making merry (dancing and playing the fiddle) in plague-ridden Walmgate.

Haunted York

York is purportedly one of the country's most haunted places, with 500 or so phantoms to its name. Examples include the girl at No. 5 College Street, who starved to death after her parents died from plague. In Bedern, where a number of orphans died at the nearby Industrial Ragged School during the 1800s, due to the negligence of the alcoholic schoolmaster, some people walking by the arch have been taken by the hand by a small child, accompanied by giggling and screaming. At St Williams' College, the ghosts of two sixteenth-century brothers appear; they murdered a priest here. One betrayed the other – the one hanged, the other went mad.

Elsewhere you can be terrified by the ghost of the philandering Duke of Buckingham in the Cock and Bottle on Skeldergate – only ever seen by women; the ghost that turns up a every funeral in All Saint's church in Pavement; an old lady, cats and Civil War soldiers haunt the Old Starre on Stonegate – it was a dressing station during the Civil War; the Grey Lady who had an affair with a York noble – she was a nun who was bricked up in a wall where the Theatre Royal now stands; the Earl of Northumberland's ghost wanders around Goodramgate looking for his head – he was executed here in 1572 for treason; Lady Alice Peckett, amongst others, haunts the Golden Fleece; a group of Roman legionaries march through the walls of the Treasurer's House; Mad Alice hovers around the eponymous lane after her hanging in 1825 for ... just being Mad Alice; Catherine Howard, the fourth wife of Henry VIII, haunts the King's Manor after her execution soon after staying there. Be scared.

York Charities

Baines Directory of 1823 tells us of the following charitable institutions:

The York Emanuel, established in the years 1781/2, for the benefit of ministers of all denominations, and the wives, widows, and children of ministers ... labouring under the misfortune of blindness or idiocy ... The Charitable Society for the relief of the distressed actually resident in York; and the Benevolent Society, for the relief of strangers in casual distress. The Lying-in Society; the Bible Society; the Church Missionary Society; the Religious Tract Society; the Hibernian Society, and the Society for the Conversion of the Jews. The Clothing Society; the Faithful Female Servant Society; and the Society for the Suppression of Vice and Immorality; the Vagrant Office, in Little Shambles, by which vagrancy is checked and the distressed traveller relieved ... The Humane Society, for the recovery of drowned persons and ... as the directions of those establishments for relieving the apparently dead, cannot be too generally promulgated, here they are:

When the body is in the room, strip and dry it; clean the mouth and nostrils; lay it on the couch, in cold weather near the fire, and cover it with a warm blanket; and gently rub it with warm flannels. In summer, expose the body to the rays of the sun; and in hot close weather, air should be freely admitted.

YOUNG CHILDREN to be put between two persons, in a warm bed.

If MEDICAL ASSISTANTS do not speedily arrive, then let the body, if DROWNED, be gently rubbed with flannel sprinkled with spirits or flour of mustard, and a heated warming-pan, covered, may be lightly moved over the back and spine.

To RESTORE BREATHING Press or pinch the mouth or nostrils exactly close, for the space of half a minute, or a minute, then let them free; but if no perceptible sign of life appears, then introduce the pipe of a bellows (when no apparatus is at hand) into *one* nostril; the *other,* and the mouth being closed, *blow into or inflate the lungs,* till the breast be a little raised; the mouth and nostrils must then be let free. Repeat this process till life appears.

TOBACCO-SMOKE, or the SMOKE of MYRRH or FRANKINCENSE, is to be thrown gently into the fundament, with a proper instrument, or the bowl of a pipe covered, so as to defend the mouth of the assistant.

The BREAST to be fomented with hot *spirits*- hot bricks or tiles, covered, andc. to be applied to the soles of the feet, and palms of the hands.

If no signs of life appear, the body is to be put into the warm bath.

Electricity is recommended to be early employed by the medical assistants, or other judicial practitioners.

HANGING. A FEW OUNCES Of BLOOD may be taken from the jugular vein, or the arm:- Cupping glasses may be applied to the head and neck :- Leeches also to the temples. The other methods of treatment, the same as recommended for the apparently drowned.

SUFFOCATION, BY NOXIOUS VAPOURS or LIGHTNING. COLD WATER to be repeatedly thrown upon the face, andc., drying the body at intervals.- IF THE BODY FEELS COLD, employ gradual *warmth*, and the above process for restoring the drowned.

The MEANS above recommended, are to be used for THREE or FOUR Hours. It is an absurd and vulgar opinion to suppose persons irrecoverable, because LIFE does not soon make its appearance.

Bleeding and Salt never to be employed, unless by the direction of the Medical Assistants.

Spiked Iron Cage 'Used for the Incarceration of Children in their Orphanages'

In June 1899, an advertisement appeared in the *Yorkshire Herald* for what promised to be a riveting night out: 'A series of lectures upon object lessons, consisting of actual instruments of torture now sanctioned by the Roman Church used by the Romanizing clergy'. Exhibits included a 'Spiked Iron Cage from the Kilburn Sisterhood, used for the Incarceration of Children in their Orphanages; hair Shirts, Rope, Steel Whips, Armlets, steel with sharp points, Cinctures'. Admission was free; questions were invited; lectures were given by members of the Protestant Alliance.

First World War

Castle Yard became an internment camp for aliens, as did a field in Leeman Road. The cattle market was a horse depot. The military requisitioned the De Grey Rooms, the Exhibition Hall and the Railway Institute. Knavesmire was a drill ground; an aerodrome was built at Copmanthorpe; 700 Belgian refugees were lodged in private houses in New Earswick and York; a canteen for travelling troops opened on York railway station; VAD hospitals opened in Clifford Street and at St John's College; stranded soldiers were given supper, bed and breakfast in the Assembly Rooms – 435 in one record night, with over 100,000 all told. A munitions factory was opened in Queen Street in two sheds hired from NER, employing 1,000, mainly women and girls. By the second week of the war, registered aliens filled the Castle Prison, with more held in a property in Leeman Road.

York, like other towns and cities, endured Zeppelin raids during the First World War, the most destructive of which occurred on the night of May 2, 1916 when eighteen bombs were unleashed on the city, destroying buildings, killing nine people and injuring forty more. Details of this raid and two others in 1916 were suppressed until 1956. Zeppelin phobia increased, and there were prosecutions of people not observing the blackout. In

September, another citizen was killed in a raid, leading to the establishment of York Patrols Committee; their controversial advice was for people to remain inside during raids; a doctor at the retreat circulated a letter on worrying levels of Zeppelinophobia. The blotches on the surviving industrial chimney on Foss Islands Road are caused by camouflage paint daubed on the chimney to deter Zeppelins. Barnitt's in Colliergate did brisk business with their Zeppelin alarms at 7s 6d each.

Second World War

York had POW camps at Naburn, the Knavesmire and at Eden Camp. In May 1940, York council tenants, who had been forbidden to keep poultry, were told they must now 'Dig for Victory' or get out. The airfield at Shipton was recommissioned to house the RAF's No. 60 Maintenance Unit; their purpose was to provide spares and collect crashed aircraft from the surrounding area. RAF Clifton opened as a civil airfield in July 1936 and was requisitioned by the RAF in 1939, initially as a relief for Linton-on-Ouse. It became a repair depot for Halifaxes operated by 83 Maintenance Unit. Clifton was badly damaged during the Baedeker raid in April 1942. After the war, it returned to civil use and was sold in the 1950s to become an industrial estate and the site for a supermarket.

Most people are familiar with the Baedecker Raid, but less is known of the other air raids and air crashes of the war and their consequences. Two questions regarding Baedecker remain unanswered to this day: why were German bombers allowed to bomb for ninety minutes unopposed before a lone RAF night-fighting Hurricane from 253 Squadron engaged? Why was York left undefended when British Intelligence knew of the impending attack through Enigma?

By April 1942, York had received 780 alerts, but luckily only a few people had been killed – on three separate occasions when stray bombs had been dropped, probably by German aircrafts lightening their loads on the way from other targets. An indication of York's immunity was that the public shelters were barely used: a large shelter near the city centre had two doors, both of which carried a notice saying, 'Key on other door'. The key was in fact in a small glass case at the end of the shelter, with a notice asking people to break the glass to obtain the key – the glass remained unbroken several days after the Baedecker raid.

7/8 June 1940

Enemy aircrafts crossed the East Coast at several points. Bombs were dropped in Yorkshire. A twenty-six-year-old fireman was killed in an incident in Stockton Lane, York.

7 August 1940

A twenty-year-old woman was killed at Osbaldwick.

1941

A Whitley bomber crash-landed, appropriately, in Landing Lane, Haxby. The crew survived.

28 April 1942

Baedecker raid.

23/24 September 1942

In an attack on York, twelve small fires were started and two people were killed.

7 December 1942

A Halifax bomber based at Rufforth, after a raid on Genoa, ran out of fuel and the pilot was forced to ditch in the Humber. Three of the crew were killed.

17/18 December 1942

At York, two gasholders were set alight and a school extensively damaged. Casualties were two fatals and four seriously injured.

9 January 1943

A Halifax bomber from Rufforth was taking off on a mining mission, when it lost power and crash landed on the A64 , just north of Copmanthorpe. The crew were uninjured.

15 September 1943

A Halifax bomber from Croft airfield was abandoned by the crew at 12.45 after the pilot's escape hatch blew off, causing him to lose control. Six of the crew baled out, one stayed with the plane and was killed when it crashed at Stillington.

18 September 1943

A Halifax from Riccall was brought in for a heavy landing and a tail wheel sheared off. Later, a Halifax from the same airfield force-landed in a field near Lissett, after the starboard inner engine caught fire. Six of the crew were injured.

7/8 October 1943

A Lancaster bomber from Linton-on-Ouse was abandoned over Hutton-le-Hole when the controls jammed. The crew parachuted to safety, but a farmer was killed when the bomber crashed at Spaunton and the bomb load blew up.

10 September 1944

A Halifax from Elvington returned from a raid on Cherbourg-Octeville with a hung-up 1,000 lb bomb. Despite the pilot shaking the aircraft the bomb was stuck fast only to fall out and explode on touch-down. Six of the crew were killed, but the pilot was blown clear and sustained injuries.

16/17 November 1944

A Halifax based at Rufforth made several attempts to land in fog. At 22.18, the bomber made another approach, but hit Grasslands farmhouse, careered across the airfield and crashed into two Halifax bombers parked there, finally hitting the airfield fire engine and bursting into flames. Six crew and two of the farmhouse occupants were killed.

28 December 1944

At 14.10 at Elvington airfield, a bomb fell from the rack of a Halifax during loading and exploded, setting off the main load and the incendiaries. Thirteen were killed and five injured.

3/4 March 1945

Seventy German night fighters attacked Halifaxes in the landing circuit at Elvington. Junkers Ju 88s and 188s penetrated the bomber stream, as the Halifaxes returned from a raid on Kamen (near Dortmund) .As the airfield lights came on and the crews switched on their navigation lights, the Luftwaffe attacked; all the airfield lights were extinguished and the Halifax crews were warned to go to their diversion airfields. One Halifax was shot down near the airfield, some ran out of fuel and crash-landed, others remained airborne until the all-clear, but most managed to land at Croft, their diversion airfield. To hide its embarrassment, Bomber Command never published any figures, but it is estimated that seventy RAF and Free-French bombers were shot down from the 210 returning from Kamen, this to the Luftwaffe's loss of only seven. One of the Luftwaffe casualties was a Junkers Ju 88G, whose pilot mistook a car's headlights for a British aircraft on the runway; the Ju 88 hit a tree during the attack and crashed at Sutton-on-Derwent. The crew were all killed.

5 March 1945

A Halifax from Linton-on-Ouse took off in freezing fog with its full bomb and fuel load. It struggled to gain height when the wings soon iced up and the plane disintegrated: the fuselage fell in Nunthorpe Grove, while an engine smashed into the kitchen of Nunthorpe Secondary School. The wireless operator baled out, but he was too low and his parachute failed to open properly; fortunately, the explosion from the crashing bomber cushioned his fall and he landed on a shed roof, seriously injured. The rest of the crew were killed, along with five civilians and eighteen injured; five houses in Nunthorpe Grove were destroyed.

April 1945

A lone German fighter strafed The Street in Haxby; one of its canon shells hit what is now the fish shop.

The Lost Streets of York

Beggergate – the bag maker's street now called Nunnery Lane.
Bookbinders' Court – after the bookshops and publishers in the area – now Minster Gates.
Cargate – former name of King Street running from Coney Street to King's Staith; it means the marshy street.
Glover Lane – a street near Petergate where glove makers worked.
Girdlegate – now Church Street; the girdle makers' street.
Graypecuntlane – nothing to do with grapes; now Grape Lane though.
Hartergate – now Friargate; the street belonging to a Viking called Hjartar.
Haymongergate – part of the Shambles: the hay merchant's street.
Ketmongergate – now St Saviourgate a Viking street: the flesh-sellers street.
Langton Lane – after Johannis de Langton; now Coffee Yard.
Lund's Court – once Mad Alice Lane – after a mad lady called Alice.
Marsh Street – a street leading to a marsh near Hungate.
Mucky Peg Lane – now Finkle Street.

Some Lost Pubs of York

Ham and Barrel (Walmgate)
Three Jolly Butchers (Church Street)
Barefoot (Micklegate)
Blue Bear (Castlegate)
Artichoke (Micklegate)
Barleycorn (Coppegate and Bedern)
Black Dog (High Ousegate)
Jolly Bacchus (High Ousegate)
George (in Bootham Bar)
Bird in Hand (demolished to make way for Exhibition Square)
Bowling Green (Groves Lane)
The Old Malt Shovel (Walmgate)
The Spiotted Dog (Walmgate)
Cricketers Arms (Tanner Row)
Cattle Market (Fawcett Street)
Cygnet (Nunnery Lane)
Ebor Vaults (Church Street)
Eagle and Child (Shambles)
Elephant and Castle (Skeldergate)
Fortunate Tar (North Street)
Froghall Tavern (Layerthorpe)
Garricks Head, Low Petergate
Hole in the Wall, next to the Chapel of St Sepulchre where the Minster Library is now
Glassmakers Arms (Fawcett Street)
Globe (Shambles)
Golden Barrel (Walmgate)
Greyhound (Spurriergate)
Ham and Firkin (Walmgate)
Hand and Heart (St Sampson's Square)
Hand and Whip (Castlegate)
Haymarket (Haymarket)
Imperial (Crichton Avenue)
Jacob's Well (Trinity Lane)
Leeds Arms (Peasholme Green)
Leopard (Coney Street)
Lion and Lamb (Blossom Street)
London Hotel (Davygate)
Londesborough Arms (No. 52 Low Petergate)
Magp (Penleys Grove Street)
Neptune (Micklegate)
Newcastle Arms (George Street)
Old Turks Head (Kings Square)
Pack Horse (Shambles)

Pack Horse (Skeldgergate)
Railway King (George Hudson Street)
Reindeer (Penleys Grove Street)
Sanctuary (No. 68 Gillygate)
Ship (No. 5 Kings Staith)
Sportsman (Hungate)
Talbot (Church Street)
Three Cups (Walmgate)
Gallows House (Tadcaster Road)
Fighting Cocks (Walmgate)
Whale Fishery (Carmelite Street)
Lottery (St Nicholas' Place)

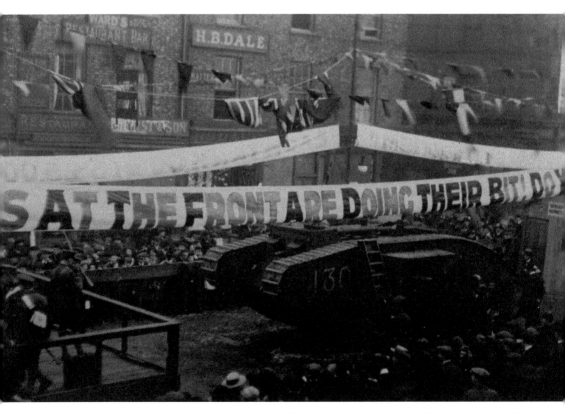

A First World War tank enlisted to help the war effort with the sale of war bonds. The tank was called 'Egbert' and went on to West Hartlepool after York. © York Press

Some York People & a Horse

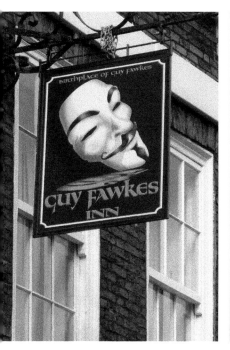
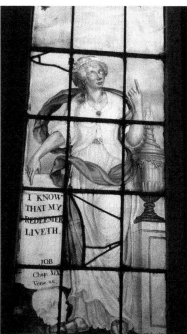
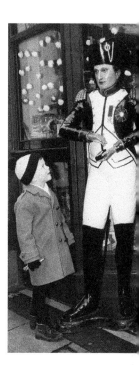

Above left: Guy Fawkes was born in this building, was baptised over the road in St Michael-le Belfrey and was an old boy of St Peter's School.

Above middle: One of William Peckitt's many beautiful windows; this one is in St Martin-cum-Gregory in Micklegate. The window is his memorial to two of his daughters, Anne and Charlotte, with the figure of Hope painted by Peckitt himself in 1792. The church is the base for The Stained Glass Centre, the national resource for the discovery and interpretation of stained glass.

Above right: Napoleon standing guard outside the Kiosk in Lendal, with David Handley of Whitby Street in 1966. © York Press

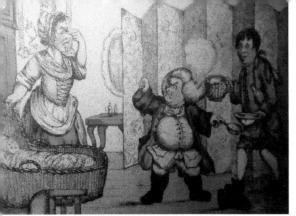
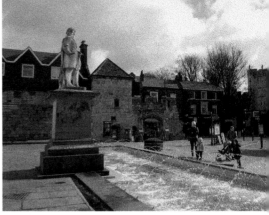

Above right: The Battle of Cataplasm from Sterne's *Life and Opinions of Tristram Shandy, Gentleman.* This depicts Dr Slop and Susannah having an almighty row; Slop's wig is on fire as he prepares to throw a cataplasm (a poultice) into Susannah's face.

Above left: William Etty surveying King's Square with Bootham Bar and the walls in front of him and St Margaret's Arch to his left.

Constantine the Great

Constantine the Great was the only Roman emperor to be proclaimed *Augustus* while in Britain in 306. He converted to Christianity in a ceremony outside the minster in 312, after seeing a vision of the cross when consulting his Roman gods before a battle. York, thereby, became an early, vital centre of Christianity. We have Constantine to thank for Christmas, for it was he who organised the first festivities celebrating Christ's birth. A marble head of Constantine was found during an excavation in Stonegate. Constantine's father, Chlorus, died in York too in 306, having been Western Emperor in AD 305/06. Septimius Severus, Rome's first black emperor, lived in York between 208 and 211; his sons, Caracalla and Geta, were declared Co-Emperors in 198 and 209. Severus died in York in 211, and received a spectacular funeral in the city, but not before he had declared York to be the capital of Britannia Inferior. Hadrian visited too.

Sweyn Forkbeard

King of Norway, Denmark and England in 1013/14, father of King Canute, is buried in York.

Yomtob of Joigny

It was Rabbi Yomtob (d. 1190) who encouraged his fellow Jews to commit suicide in Clifford's Tower during the massacre; Yomtob himself killed sixty of his comrades once they had killed their own wives and children.

Andrew de Barclay

Found guilty of conspiracy with the Scots in the early fourteenth century, de Barclay could have been in no doubt as to the finality of his death when he was told that he will be 'hanged, drawn and beheaded; that your heart and bowels and entrails, when come your traitorous thoughts, be torn out and burnt to ashes, and that the ashes be scattered to the winds; that your body be cut into four quarters'.

One of these was displayed on the bridge at York while the others went to Newcastle, Carlisle and Shrewsbury; his head was stuck on London Bridge.

Philippa of Hainault

Philippa of Hainault, a fifteen-year-old princess, who spoke both Flemish and French, came to York to marry Edward III on 24 January 1328. Queen Philippa often travelled with her husband, and was present at the defeat of the Scots at the Battle of Neville's Cross (1346) and the capture of Calais (1347), where she pleaded for the lives of the Six Burghers, shown in Rodin's marvellous sculpture in Calais (and its replica near the Houses of Parliament). Less well-known is the fact that she successfully pleaded for the lives of the carpenters who had made a stand, which collapsed at a tournament she attended in York. Queen's college, Oxford was founded in her honour. Hainault is in modern-day Belgium.

Iucundus the Monk

Iucundus' joining the fifteenth-century monks of St Leonard's was a bit of a mistake – the well-named novice was somewhat bibulous and something of a party animal. His chosen life of asceticism did not sit well with him, so he compromised and decided to live a life of austerity all year long – apart from on one day. This day happened to coincide with York Fair – never an abstemious event – to which Iucundus repaired and truly let down what was left of his hair. The following day he was wheeled home in a barrow and tried – his punishment was to be walled up without delay in the priory cellar. His struggle to save himself resulted in the wall collapsing, through which he tumbled into St Mary's Abbey immediately next door; he soon became a Benedictine monk there, a paragon of sobriety. One year or so later, Iucundus was appointed keeper of the cellar; unfortunately, this also served as a wine cellar and, soon after his appointment, Iucundus was found comatose at the wrong end of a barrel of claret: his punishment was, again, to be immured at the scene of the crime, which happened to be the exact place through which Iucundus had tumbled through from the priory next door. His former colleagues heard the commotion he made, tore down the walls and were confronted by the miracle that was Iucundus. So stupefied where they that they made Iucundus Prior of St Leonard's.

Miles Coverdale

Born in York in 1488, as Bishop of Exeter, he made the first translation of the Bible into English in 1539, printed and published it.

Catherine Howard

Fifth wife of Henry VIII, she came with him to York in 1541 and allegedly consummated her affair with Thomas Culpepper in the rose garden of the King's Manor. Jane Seymour was destined to be crowned Queen in the minster, but died giving birth to Edward VI in 1537.

Robert Aske

One of the leaders of the Pilgrimage of Grace who was hanged in chains from Clifford's Tower for his troubles by Henry VIII in 1537. He died a slow death a week later; his body was left there for a year as a warning to other potential traitors. The Pilgimage was a popular uprising in the autumn of 1536 in protest against Henry VIII's s break with the Catholic Church, the Dissolution of the Monasteries and the policies of Thomas Cromwell.

Thomas Stafford

Committed treason in 1557 with others against Queen Mary; the corporation funded the 'expense of boiling, carving and setting up of the carcasses of the late traitors about this city, amounting to 12s 6d'.

Dolly Dilby – the Devil's Whore

Hanged for witchcraft in 1586, she admitted to being paid ten shillings a time for services to the devil.

Guy Fawkes

Fawkes was born just off Low Petergate, baptised at St Michael-le-Belfry and a pupil at St Peter's. As Capt. Guido Fawkes. he had a distinguished military record, and his expertise with explosives led the Plotters to recruit him in their attempt to assassinate James I. Though he is still burnt in effigy on 5th November ('Plot Night' as it is called in parts of Yorkshire) no guy is ever burnt on the bonfire at St Peter's.

Jane Hodson – Serial Mother

Jane and Phineas Hodson had no fewer than twenty-four children between them before she died in childbirth aged thirty-eight in 1636. She is buried in York Minster.

John William Nevison – Swift Nick

In 1684, at dawn, witnesses saw Nevison commit a robbery in Gad's Hill London. Fifteen hours later he arrived in Museum Gardens on horseback and engaged the Lord Mayor, who was playing bowls, in conversation. His alibi thus established, Swift Nick was acquitted. He was, nevertheless, beyond rehabilitation and was imprisoned at York before his execution for robbery where his leg irons weighed 28 lb.

John Moore – the Only Black Freeman of the City of York

Moore, a native Moor, was the only black man on York's Freemen's Rolls – bluntly, albeit accurately, listed as John Moore – 'blacke'. Moore paid two amounts – 20 nobles (equivalent to 13s 6d) to the Common Chamber of the City of York and £4 to the city council – for this privilege in 1687.

Elizabeth Robinson

Elizabeth Robinson was born in Gray's Court in 1718; she founded the Blue Stocking Club 'where literary topics were to be discussed, but politics, gossip and card-playing were barred'. Blue stockings the world over are forever in her debt.

Maj.-Gen. James Wolfe

The Wolfe family lived at the Black Swan in Peasholme Green from 1724 to 1726, although Wolfe was not born at the inn. James Wolfe (1727–59) went on to a distinguished military career culminating in victory at the Battle of Quebec in 1759.

Dr John Burton

One time resident in the Red House, and the model for Laurence Sterne's Dr Slop in *The Life and Times of Tristram Shandy*, as depicted in Hogarth's frontispiece for the first edition. Burton, a medical doctor educated at Cambridge, Leiden and Rheims, also authored the unfinished *Monasticon Eboracense*, an ecclesiastical history of Yorkshire, in 1758. He was incarcerated in York Castle after his involvement in the 1745 Jacobite Rebellion, as 'a suspicious person to His Majesty's government'. There is a memorial to him in Holy Trinity church, Micklegate.

Alicia Meynell

The first female jockey to compete in a horse race against men at the Knavesmire in 1755 when she rode Vingarella side-saddle. Victory, though, had to wait until the following year when she won on Louisa, again at the Knavesmire.

William Peckitt

William Peckitt was born in Husthwaite in 1731, one of England's foremost glass painters and stained-glass makers – in fact he is widely regarded as the most prominent and prolific glazier of his day and responsible for keeping the craft alive in the eighteenth century. Patrons included the Dean of York and Horace Walpole with commissions at New College, Oxford and the cathedrals at Exeter, Lincoln and Ripon. The family moved to York around 1750, where William worked in his father's glove making business before setting himself up as a glass painter in Colliergate. He died in 1795 and is buried in St Martin-cum-Gregory where Mary, his wife and assistant, made a memorial window to him. His *Commission Book* is the earliest surviving account of glass painting and includes 315 works ranging from sash windows to cathedral windows.

John Goodricke

Born in Groningen on 17 September 1764, he lived most of his life at the Treasurer's House. At the age of five, he contracted scarlet fever, which left him profoundly deaf and dumb. Notwithstanding, Goodricke became an accomplished astronomer; the plaque outside his home reads:

> From a window in the Treasurer's House, City of York, the young deaf and dumb astronomer John Goodrick, who was elected a fellow of the Royal Society at the age of 21, observed the periodicity of the star ALGOL and discovered the variation of CEPHEL and other stars thus laying the foundation of modern measurement of the Universe.

He died aged twenty-one. His cousin was Edward Piggott (1753–1825), another gifted York astronomer, who worked with Goodricke in their observatory behind the Black Horse Inn in Bootham.

Sir John Vanbrugh

Sir John, dramatist, member of the Kit Kat Club and architect of Blenheim Palace and Castle Howard, married Henrietta Maria Yarburgh of Heslington Hall in St Lawrence's church on 14 January 1719. St Lawrence was rebuilt in 1883 and is the city's largest parish church. The church is huge and is often described as the 'Minster without the walls.'

John Carr

Born in 1723, Carr was Lord Mayor of York in 1770 and 1785. He lived on his estate at Askham Richard for most of his adult life. He designed the Crescent at Buxton; racecourse grandstands at York, Doncaster and Nottingham, prisons at Wakefield and Northallerton, Greta Bridge, Constable Burton Hall and Harewood House. His crowning achievement is the magnificent Fairfax House in Castlegate, York.

Whistlejacket

The winner of the first race to pass the new Knavesmire grandstand, designed by John Carr in 1755. Whistlejacket achieved eternal fame when he was painted by George Stubbs; the painting hangs in The National Gallery

Beilby Porteus and the Plight of the Negro Slave

Born in York in 1731, the youngest but one of nineteen children, Porteus became Bishop of Chester and then London. He was an active campaigner against slavery, criticising the church's apathy regarding the plight of negro slaves in its Codrington Estates on Barbados in his *The Civilisation, Improvement and Conversion of the Negroe Slaves in the British West-India Islands Recommended.*

Elizabeth Boardingham – Burnt at the Stake for Treason

In 1776, Elizabeth Boardingham was burnt at the stake at Tyburn in York, the last person to suffer this fate in Yorkshire. In killing her husband, Elizabeth was considered to have broken the 'natural hierarchy', which ranked men above women. Her crime, therefore, was not murder but petty treason, which carried the more severe sentence of burning at the stake. Her accomplice was her lover, Thomas Aikney, who hanged; rumour has it that, as they parted at Tyburn, she asked him for a kiss and he refused. Maybe he had other things on his mind?

George Stubbs

George Stubbs (1724–1806) had come to York to learn his anatomy and found work teaching medical students in the first York Medical School before taking up comparative anatomy and painting his famous horses.

Mary Morris and the Rejection of George Washington

Mary Morris (1730–1825) came to York in 1783 as a refugee after the American War of Independence; like her husband Roger Morris, she is buried in St Saviour's church. Roger fought with George Washington at the Battle of Monongahela in the French and Indian War. Mary met Washington soon after – she was 'an imperious brunette ... adored by half the officers in New York ... an elegant woman'. She is said to have been the model for James Fennimore Cooper's heroine in *The Spy*. George Washington took a shine to Mary and proposed. Without the benefit of hindsight, Mary denied Washington and chose Roger Morris instead – something of a ladies' man.

Dr John Snow, Cholera and Princess Beatrice of Battenberg

Snow was born 15 March 1813 in North Street, and apprenticed to a surgeon at the age of fourteen. He was a pioneer in anesthesia and correctly calculated dosages of chloroform and ether as an anesthetic. He was the anaesthetist at the birth of Queen Victoria's last of nine children, Beatrice Mary Victoria Feodore, born in 1856 and later Princess Beatrice of Battenberg. Snow is most famous, though, for his ground-breaking work on cholera; he rejected the belief that cholera was transmitted through the air – the 'miasma' (bad air) theory, arguing instead that it was orally transmitted. He published his findings in an essay, *On the Mode of Communication of Cholera*, in 1849, and proved his theory in 1854 when cholera broke out in Soho. Snow identified a water pump in Broad (now Broadwick) Street as the source of the disease and had the handle of the pump removed. Cases of cholera slumped, but scepticism prevailed and Snow's theory was not widely accepted until the 1860s.

Napoleon Bonaparte

Napoleon arrived in York in 1822, one year after his death on St Helena. He stood sentinel first in Bridge Street for 153 years outside Mrs Clarke's tobacconist and then outside Judith Thorpe's tobacconists in Lendal, to whom letters were addressed simply as 'Napoleon, York' and were delivered. In full uniform, he is proffering a snuffbox to passers-by; Napoleon liked his snuff. He is carved out of a solid piece of oak and is the only known survivor of three made, each selling for £50. Apparently, during the Second World War, he ended up in the River Ouse, courtesy of allied soldiers garrisoned in York; he was recovered none the worse at Naburn Lock and is now safely accommodated in the Merchant Adventurer's Hall. Another Napoleonic connection with York is the elm tree next to the water tower on Lendal bridge; this was grown from a cutting taken from Napoleon's grave on St Helena.

Sir Walter Scott

Part of Scott's *Ivanhoe* (1820) is set in York. Scott volunteered to walk the 193 miles from Edinburgh to York in a futile bid to save the barbican on Micklegate Bar from destruction.

John Peacock Needham

A Lendal surgeon heavily preoccupied with the first cholera epidemic. When it ended in 1833, Needham worked hard to discover more about the disease and published his *Facts and Observations Related to the Disease Commonly Called Cholera as it has Recently Prevailed in the City of York.*

General 'Stonewall' Jackson

Thomas Jonathan 'Stonewall' Jackson (d. 1863), Confederate General in the American Civil War, visited York in the 1830s. *The Times* reported in his obituary: 'He dwelt with great animation upon the vibration of the air produced by the deep notes of the organ in York Minster...it is rare to find in a Presbyterian such appreciation and admiration of Cathedral magnificence'.

Nathaniel Whittock

Whittock produced the celebrated 'map' of York in 1856. He had already produced views of Oxford, Melbourne, Hull and London, three times. In 1839, he wrote the world's first photography manual.

Joseph Rougier

A maker of drinking horns, combs and lanterns from 1823 until 1931. Rougier was descended from a Huguenot family of wigmakers and hairdressers and gave his name to the street near his Tanner Row works; another was George Steward and Son in Blossom Street. Rougier's son, Joseph (d. 1842), was appointed Manufacturer of Ornamental Horn Shavings to Queen Victoria in 1837. The industry began to recede from 1796 when mechanisation was introduced.

Frank Green

Eccentric owner of the Treasurer's House. Green chained himself to the pillars of the arch linking Goodramgate and Deangate when, in 1901, the council threatened to demolish it. Green went on to pay for the upkeep of the arch. He had his groceries sent up to York from London, he hired a French chef to cook for him, he slept in fresh Jaeger linen sheets every day, and sent his laundry to London every week by train. He ordered his staff to wrap all the coal in the house individually in newspaper because he hated the sound of it rattling in the scuttles.

William Etty RA

The 1911 statue of York artist William Etty (1787–1849) stands proudly outside York City Art Gallery, the home of many of his, often controversial and to some, shocking, paintings. Etty founded the York School of Design in 1842, later the York School of Art. We have much to thank him for when it comes to the surviving walls, bars and buildings of York. His sonorous letter to the city's Corporation vandals resonates to this day: 'Beware how you destroy your antiquities, guard them with religious care! They are what give you a decided character and superiority over other provincial cities. You have lost much, take care of what remains.' Etty first exhibited at the Royal Academy in 1811, becoming an Academician in 1828. He is buried in St Olave's, Marygate.

Anne and Charlotte Brontë

Stayed at the George Inn in Coney Street en route to Scarborough in 1849. Anne was awed by the grandeur of the minster; she died in Scarborough.

Queen Victoria

In 1854, when Victoria, Albert and five of their children stopped off at York for a meal on the way to Balmoral, there were local complaints about the expense of such a short visit: £483 13s 7d – the meal was never eaten. Victoria got wind of the disquiet and was so unamused that she never visited the city again in the remaining forty-seven years of her reign. The *Visit York* website takes up the story:

> She had stated that this was a private visit, to be without ceremony. But the city council laid on a military display and erected stands for spectators; the Queen's temper was not improved when some of these collapsed and there was an unseemly scuffle. When the Queen eventually went to the Royal Station Hotel for her lunch, she was shocked to be presented with the bill to pay. She got up and said she would never visit York again, and never did. Whenever the Royal Train passed through York thereafter, she always made sure the blinds were firmly pulled down!

Delightful as it is, the story is a myth. Victoria had first visited the city as a princess in 1849. She passed through York eighteen more times, getting out of the train on ten occasions.

George Cadbury – No 'Indolent and Wayward' Men

Cadbury served a three-year apprenticeship with Rowntrees' at the Pavement shop before he joined his family firm in Bournville in 1857. He would have quickly become familiar with the regime there: the rules of the Pavement shop were uncompromising, as set out in the elder Joseph's 1852 *Memoranda of Business and Household Arrangements*:

> The object of the Pavement establishment is business. The young men who enter it...are expected to contribute ... in making it successful ... it affords a full opportunity for any painstaking, intelligent young man to obtain a good practical acquaintance with the tea and grocery trades ... the place is not suitable for the indolent and wayward.

'Henry Hunnings? Who's Calling?'

In 1878, Henry Hunnings, the curate at Bolton Percy with a passion for his hobby, electricity, filed the patent for the granular carbon microphone – a system still used in telephones today. His design improved on that developed by Edison, was successfully tested between York and Darlington and became the most popular telephone transmitter in face of competition from designs by Edison and Alexander Graham Bell; it remains the world's best today.

Henrietta Eliza Vaughan Stannard (1856–1911)

Born in The Cottage, Trinity Lane, the only daughter of Henry Vaughan Palmer (d. 1877), rector of St Margaret's, York. Stannard went to Bootham House School after which, in 1874, she assumed the *nom de plume*, 'Violet Whyte', writing for the *Family Herald*. In 1881, she published *Cavalry Life,* a collection of regimental sketches and, in 1883, *Regimental Legends.* Both were written under the name of John Strange Winter, a character in one of her stories; her (male) publisher refused to bring out the books under a feminine pseudonym while the public assumed the author to be a cavalry officer. In 1885, *Bootle's Baby: A Story of the Scarlet Lancers* was published in the *Graphic,* selling two million copies in ten years. John Ruskin described John Strange Winter as 'the author to whom we owe the most finished and faithful rendering ever yet given of the character of the British soldier'. She was first president of the Writers' Club (1892), and was president of the Society of Women Journalists from 1901 to 1903.

Joseph Hansom and his 'Gondola of London'

Joseph Aloysius Hansom (1842–1900), the architect and inventor of the Patent Safety Cabriolet that bears his name, was born at No. 114 Micklegate and christened in the Bar Convent chapel. He suffered from severe depression and shot himself in his office on 27 May 1900. A pub in Market Street was named after him. Architecturally, Hansom's best-known work is probably the majestic neoclassical Birmingham Town Hall. The Hansom Cab was so common a sight that Disraeli called it 'the gondola of London'.

Joseph Rowntree – Social Worker

Here are just some of the less familiar good causes supported by Joseph Rowntree (1836–1925) and Quakers in York: York Anti Slavery Society; York Association for the Prosecution of Felons and Villains; York Society for the Prevention and Discouragement of Vice and Profaneness;

Society to Assist the Labouring and Poor Classes of York; the Mission to the Indians; Dr Choke's Society for Promoting Schools in Africa; Society for Promoting Permanent and Universal Peace; Society for Promoting the Education of Native Females in India; the Society for the Prevention of Youthful Depravity; Female Temperance Association; York Society for the Encouragement of Faithful Female Servants; York Meeting Sewing Circle.

WA Evelyn

In 1905, Dr W.A. Evelyn (1860–1935) organized an exhibition in York City Art Gallery – *York Views and Worthies,* comprising images of York. He started his famous series of lectures in 1909 and in 1934, he donated his huge collection of pictures to the city to be held in the Gallery. A fervent defender of the city's heritage and member of York Architectural and York Archaeological Society (YAYAS), Dr Evelyn campaigned tirelessly against the destruction or ruination of many of York's finest sights. *The Evelyn Collection* is accessible through YAYAS, www.yayas.free-online.co.uk

The RMS *Titanic* victims

The *Titanic* claimed the lives of two York men when it sank in 1912: J Foley, forty-four-year-old storekeeper, and C Stagg, thirty-seven-year-old steward.

Sir Francis Terry – Saint, Knight and Perfectionist

Knighted in 1936, Terry was a popular character. He would often bring in flowers from the garden for the office girls; quality, though, could never be compromised. Peter Terry relates the story of Sir Francis officiating at a tasting session one day, when he exclaimed, 'I have never seen such stuff!' and threw the samples out of the open window to be gathered up later by ground staff. On the other hand, he could show real generosity: for the trip to London to receive his knighthood all the employees' works numbers were put in a hat and twelve were drawn out; these lucky dozen stayed at the Savoy and took in a show at the Drury Lane Theatre.

Robert Thompson

Thompson's distinctive mice can be seen in the archway of King William's College and in the minster.

L. S. Lowr

Every year between 1950 and 1962, an artist was paid £50 to produce a picture of York. Lowry's painting of Clifford's Tower is one of the results. York City Art Gallery is currently undergoing a radical two-year refurbishment.

Frankie Howerd

Francis Alick Howerd, master of the camp and the double entendre was born in York in 1917 at No. 53 Hartoft Street, Fulford Road; a wall plaque at the Grand Opera House celebrates his life, which ended in 1992. His mother worked at Terry's. Howerd changed his name from Howard because he believed there to be too many funny Howards around already.

Charles Whiting, aka Leo Kessler

Writer and military historian of some 350 books of fiction and non-fiction, under his own name and pseudonyms including Leo Kessler. He was born in the Bootham area in 1926 and was a pupil at Nunthorpe Grammar School, leaving aged sixteen to join the army. He is best-known locally for his *York Blitz* (also published as *Fire Over York*) about the Baedecker Raid on York; his most controversial work is *Hemingway Goes To War*, about the exploits of Ernest Hemingway during the Second World War.

Francis Matthews

Francis Matthews (b. 1927) went to St George's RC Primary School, then St Michael's Jesuit College in Leeds. In 1967, Matthews was the voice of Captain Scarlet for Gerry and Sylvia Anderson's *Captain Scarlet and the Mysterons*.

The Right Honourable Dr (John) Vincent Cable MP

Born 9 May 1943 in York, into a working-class Tory family, his father, Len, worked for Rowntree and Edith, his mother, for Terry's. He too attended Nunthorpe Grammar School and then Fitzwilliam College, Cambridge, where he initially studied natural sciences, later switching to economics. Cable's first wife was Olympia Rebelo, whom he met 'in the unromantic setting of a York mental hospital where we happened to be working as nurses during a summer vacation'. Olympia Cable died soon after the 2001 election; in 2004 he married Rachel Wenban Smith. He wears the wedding rings from both of his marriages.

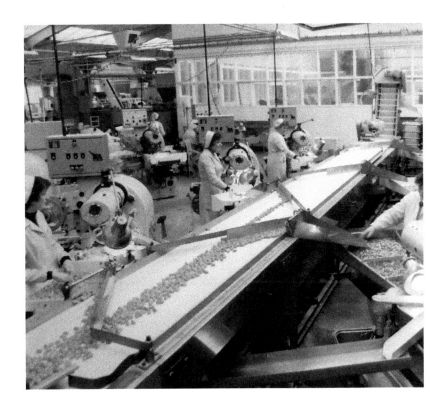

A production line at Craven's, York's other confectionery company.
© York Press

Written York

Alcuin
From the introduction to his eighth-century book *On the Saints of the Church of York*:
'My heart is set to praise my home And briefly tell the ancient cradling Of York's famed city through the charms of verse...'

Domesday York
York's entry tells us about the 1,418 houses in 1086 with such detail as 'Odo the Crossbowman has three dwellings, of Forne and Orne ... Landric the carpenter has ten and half dwellings which the sheriff assigned to him'.

William of Malmesbury
Writing in 1125, the father of British history shows us how little has really changed in 900 years with regard to the North/South divide:

> Next in rank after Canterbury is York ... almost everything about the language of the North, and particularly of the people of York, is so crude and discordant that we southerners cannot understand it. This is because they are near to barbarian peoples [the Scots] and far from the English kings.

Edward III
Edward III married Philippa of Hainault in the minster; he was not impressed, as this letter of 1332 makes clear: 'detesting the abominable smell abounding in the said city more than in any other city in the realm from dung and manure and other filth and dirt'. He goes on to order the mayor to clean up the city.

John Leland
John Leland visited York in 1534 and gave a very detailed account: 'And thens over Fosse by a bridge to the castel. Fosse bridge of [5] arches above it; Laithorpbridge on Fosse of 3 arches. Monke bridge on Fosse of 5 arches without Goodrome gate.'

William Camden
In 1586, Camden wrote in his Latin *Britannia*, the first guide book to Britain:

> York is the second city of England, the most beautiful of this region and indeed the hole north, as well as its principal fortress . It is pleasant, large, and strongly fortified, adorned with private as well as public buildings, crammed with riches and with people...

William Shakespeare
Heads and quarters of traitors were routinely displayed on the top of Micklegate Bar, most famously Richard Duke of York after the Battle of Wakefield in 1460, prompting Shakespeare to write: 'Off with his head and set it on York's gates; so York did overlook the town of York'

(Queen Margaret, *Henry VI*). The opening lines of *Richard III* refer to 'the sun of York', a punning reference to the sun badge of Edward IV. Ann Vavasour was the mysterious 'dark' lady of Shakespeare's Sonnets.

James Ryther

Ryther here reports back to Lord Burghley, chief advisor to Elizabeth I. Ryther was a fan, neither of the people of York, nor of the city itself. He remarked on a strange infatuation with the place of cows in York society and was particularly disappointed by the local beer and the stinginess of York people:

> Their usury ... is more than Jewish...for all their use of drinking inordinately, yet [there is] no faculty as a common brewer in their city by which their beer is not good or wholesome. Their ale is mingled with resin to make it strong, in some parts with urine ... the magistrates are so simple.

Richard Norwood

Norwood, a 'reader in the Mathematicks' published his *A Sea-Mans Practice* in 1637, detailing the painstaking journey he made on foot, from London to the 'Cittye of Yorke'. It took him two years, carrying with him a 90-ft chain, a 5-ft sextant and a magnetic compass. His aim? To determine accurately the 'distance occupied by one degree along a great circle of the Earth'. Assuming he took Sundays off, he would have covered 1,700 feet per day, making 10,300 measurements with his chain. Ever since Ptolemy in AD 100, the accepted distance for one degree was 60 miles; after Norwood it was extended, by 16 per cent. Norwood had a significant influence on Sir Isaac Newton's *Philisophiae Naturalis Principia Mathematica* of 1686. Norwood's book was reprinted five times.

Celia Fiennes

The intrepid lady traveller journeyed the length and breadth of the country, often with only one or two maids in attendance; she visited York in 1697. This is how she described the River 'Ouise' and the mean streets of York, in her journal *Great Journey to Newcastle and to Cornwall*:

> it bears Great Barges, it Looks muddy, its full of good ffish. We Eate very good Cod fish and Salmon and that at a pretty Cheape rate, tho' we were not in the best jnn for the Angel is the best in Cunny Streete. The houses are very Low and as indifferent as in any Country town and the Narrowness of ye Streetes makes it appear very mean.

Francis Drake

Drake (1696–1771) was an eminent York surgeon at York County Hospital and author of the landmark *Eboracum, or the History and Antiquities of the City of York*. Some things have changed, some have not, as this extract shows:

> Our streets are kept clean, and lighted with lamps, every night in the winter season; and so regular are the inhabitants, to their hours of rest, that it is rare to meet any person, after ten or eleven at night ... the common people are very well made and proportioned...

the women are remarkably handsome; it being taken notice of by strangers that they observe more pretty faces in York than in any other place ... the better sort talk the English language in perfection at York. Without the affected tone and mincing speech of the southern people.

He became a member of the Royal Society; debts landed him in a debtor's prison until bailed out by his patron.

Daniel Defoe

'There is abundance of good company here, and abundance of good families live here, for the sake of the good company and cheap living; a man converses here with all the world as effectually as at London.' This is how Daniel Defoe generously described York in his '*A Tour Thro' The Whole Island Of Great Britain*', 1724. He described Ouse Bridge as 'near 70 foot in diameter; it is, without exception, the greatest in England, some say it's as large as the Rialto at Venice, though I think not'. With the distinct advantage of seeing things from the outside, Defoe liked the prison, describing it as 'the most stately and complete of any in the whole kingdom, if not in Europe'. Defoe's *Robinson Crusoe* opens with 'I was born in the year 1862, in the city of York, of a good family...'

Laurence Sterne

Sterne (1713–68) is famous for his, *The Life and Opinions of Tristram Shandy, Gentleman*, and *A Sentimental Journey Through France and Italy*. He was also an Anglican clergyman with a vicarship at Sutton-on-the-Forest, a living at Stillington and was a prebendary of York Minster, lodging at Hildyard's in Stonegate. Sterne married Elizabeth Lumley, who lived in College Street. His satire, *A Political Romance* (1759), exposed political infighting at the minster. Sterne died of pleurisy in London in 1768; he is buried in the churchyard in Coxwold, but only after a circuitous journey ... having been originally interred in St George's churchyard, Hanover Square, London. His body was snatched by 'resurrection men' for use in medical dissection at Cambridge University. The cadaver was recognised by the Professor of Anatomy there, who fainted when he saw it on the table and had it hastily reburied. In 1969, the Lawrence Sterne Society obtained permission to remove Sterne's remains to Coxwold for reburial. Dr John Burton was the model for Dr Slop in *Tristram Shandy*; he once lived in the Red House; Burton was a gynaecologist and medical author whose books included *An Essay Towards a Complete System of Midwifery*.

Tobias Smollett

The Expedition of Humphry Clinker, published in 1771, features the Assembly Rooms: somewhere sumptuous where the local gentry could play dice and cards, dance and take tea. Smollett was not impressed: 'the company, on a ball night, must look like an assembly of fantastic fairies, revelling by moonlight among the columns of a Grecian temple'. In his *Travels* – letters sent home from Boulogne, Paris, Nice, and other places, he saw in Durham Cathedral and York Minster, gloomy and depressing piles.

William Alexander and Scott's Dr Dryasdust

One of York's earliest booksellers and printers; he refused to publish secular novels, considering them far too ephemeral. His self-censorship was to cost him dear. Walter Scott

(1771–1832), while researching *Ivanhoe,* came to York and visited Alexander's bookshop where he suggested Alexander might publish his book. Alexander declined, saying 'I esteem your friendship, but I fear thy books are too worldly for me to print'. He paid for his rebuff, though, as the bookseller is thought to be the boring Dr Dryasdust to whom Scott dedicated *Ivanhoe.* Castlegate provides the setting for Walter Scott's *The Severn Stars* where Jeanie Deans stayed en route to London in *Heart of Midlothian.*

The Cries of York

York, like other cities, had its own repertoire of cries. Some of these were compiled in a penny book and published by J. Kendrew of Colliergate in 1811, 'for the amusement of good children'. Typical are: 'Threepence a quart, Ripe Goosberries, Ripe gooseberries at York you'll buy, As cheap as cheap can be, Of many sorts you hear the cry, Pray purchase sir of me', and, 'A list of horses that's to start On Knavesmire, and each name; With riders that are dressed so smart, Anxious the prize to claim'.

Sydney Smith

'At the turn of the nineteenth century, the streets of York required some skill in this art [coach driving]. My father once exclaiming to one of the principal tradesmen there, "why, Mr Brown, your streets are the narrowest in Europe"'.

Charles Dickens

On one of his visits to York in 1838, Dickens describes in his *Letters*, a visit to his friend, John Camidge, organist at the minster, who showed him around. Dickens was particularly struck by 'the deep organ's bursting heart throb through the shivering air' and the Five Sisters Window. Dickens' story about the window appears in *Nicholas Nickleby* as the *Five Sisters of York.* The first reading was given in York at the long gone Festival Concert Rooms in Blake Street; the *Yorkshire Gazette* tells us that Dickens 'elicited unbounded applause and sent his audience home delighted'. Mr Micawber from *David Copperfield*, too, finds his origins in York, based as he is on a Richard Chicken, a feckless character who, in 1847, worked in the same railway office as Albert Dickens, Charles' railway engineer brother. Chicken was also an actor and at one time a self-styled Professor of Elocution and lecturer on defective annunciation.

Wilkie Collins

A frequent visitor, he set his 1862 novel, *No Name*, in the city, describing a walk along the walls by Captain Wragge as 'one of the most striking scenes which England can show ... the majestic west front of York Minster soared over the city and caught the last brightest light of heaven on the summits of its lofty towers'. On the other hand, his description of Skeldergate is less uplifting: 'dingy warehouses and joyless private residences of red brick'.

Elizabeth Gaskell

The Mansion House is famously threatened with being burnt to the ground in Gaskell's *Sylvia's Lovers* (1863), if the Mayor, in 1777, failed to satisfy the demands of the press-gang.

W. H. Auden

Wystan Hugh Auden was born at No. 54, Bootham on 21 February 1907; his father, G. A. Auden, was Medical Officer for York and author of *The Gild of Barber Surgeons of the City of York*.

J. B. Priestley

In 1933, Priestley wrote in his *English Journey*: 'York is, of course, the guide-book man's paradise, and not without good reason, for if you want the past, here it is, weighing tons.'

Opposite (clockwise from top left):
Episode II, Scene VI AD 306. The coming of the first Christians while Constantine the Great is offering sacrifice at the heathen altar.

Episode V, Scenes 4–7 (*clockwise from top left*): Josias – a Jew, 1190; Thomas Plantagenet, 1390; Sir William and Lady Selby – first Lord Mayor and Lady Mayoress of York, 1398; Edward III, 1328; and Philippa of Hainault.

Banners of the Old Craft Guilds and Companies (*clockwise from top left*): millers, or milners; curriers; pewterers; skinners; tallow chandlers; vintners; merchant taylors.

The Final Tableau; York, New York and sixteen other Yorks.

Characters (*clockwise from top left*): Queen Ethelburga, King Harold, Morcar of Mercia, Canadia, Venisus.

The Mystery Plays

The following images of the York Pageant of 1909 were originally published in the limited edition *Book of the York Pageant, 1909*, published and printed by Ben Johnson of Micklegate in 1909.

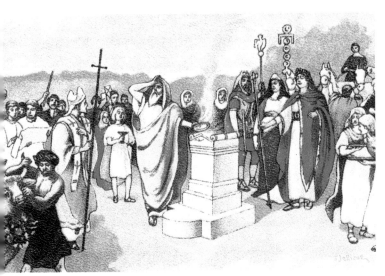

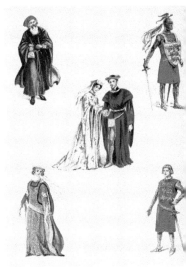

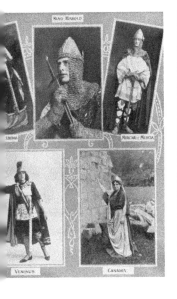

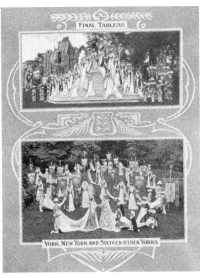

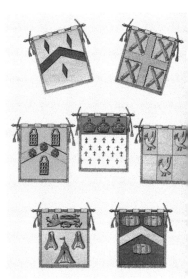

The Mystery Plays are not included in this book of secrets and mysteries because there is nothing at all mysterious about them. The word 'mystery' in this context means a 'trade' or 'craft' in medieval English; it is also, of course, a religious truth or rite. The Mystery Plays were revived during the 1951 York Festival of the Arts; they were performed on a fixed stage in the Museum Gardens – it was not until 1954 that a wagon play, *The Flood,* toured the streets. The 1951 production was the most popular Festival of Britain event in the country, with over 26,000 people seeing the plays. The medieval plays were traditionally sponsored by the city's craft guilds – ninety-two separate trade associations - with an inclusive cast of 600 performers and 120 torchbearers, including the Lord Mayor, members of the council and ordinary folk; songs were in Latin. Richard II was in the audience in 1397; the last performance was in 1569. Nowadays, since 1994, the medieval *Corpus Christi* plays are produced every four years, with the next due in 2016, by the York Guilds and Companies. *The Creation* to the *Last Judgement* is paraded through the streets on pageant wagons as actors perform selections from the forty-eight high points of Christian history at twelve playing stations designated by the city banners, with one guild taking responsibility for one episode. The sole surviving manuscript of the York plays, from around 1465, is in the British Library.

York Pageant 1909

The 1909 pageant was produced as a dramatic representation of the city's history in seven episodes from 800 BC to AD 1644. Everything – every costume, every banner, every suit of armour – was designed and produced by the people of York over two years. More than 2,500 actors took part, with dancers and soldiers from the 2nd Yorkshire Regiment and the 5th Lancers, along with 103 horses.

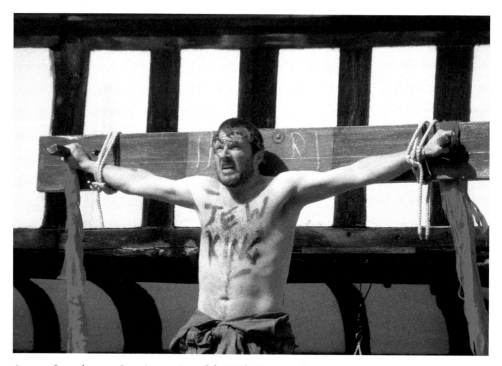

A scene from the 2014 Interim staging of the York Mystery Plays.